MAKING DESIGNER
JEWELRY WITH HARDWARE, GEMS, AND BEADS

MAKING DESIGNER
JEWELRY WITH HARDWARE, GEMS, AND BEADS

Nicole Noelle Sherman

BEVERLY MASSACHUSETTS

QUARRY BOOKS

First published in the United States of America by
Quarry Books, a member of
Quayside Publishing Group
100 Cummings Center
Suite 406-L
Beverly, Massachusetts 01915-6101
Telephone: (978) 282-9590
Fax: (978) 283-2742
www.quarrybooks.com

Library of Congress Cataloging-in-Publication Data

Sherman, Nicole Noelle.
  Making designer jewelry with hardware, gems, and beads / Nicole Noelle
Sherman.
     p. cm.
  ISBN 1-59253-422-8
  1. Jewelry making. 2. Wire craft. I. Title.
  TT212.S543 2008
  739.27--dc22

                                                2007048906
ISBN-13: 978-1-59253-422-7
ISBN-10: 1-59253-422-8

10 9 8 7 6 5 4 3 2 1

Design: Emily Brackett/Visible Logic
All photography by Lexi Boeger with the exception of exteriors and interiors of hardware
stores by William H. Sherman.

Illustrations: Judy Love

Printed in Singapore

TO ALL OF THE GREAT OLD HARDWARE STORES STILL IN BUSINESS.

May they survive, thrive, and continue to inspire! To all the grandfathers I have known or just imagined.

CONTENTS

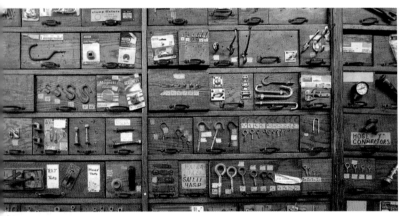

INTRODUCTION

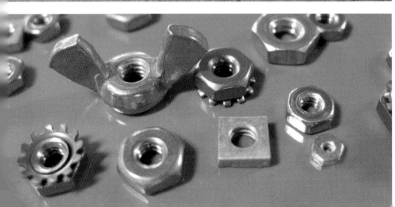

I grew up in a classic New England small town, white clapboard houses with dogs and kids running loose. The center of the village, as we called it, had a church, a community center, an elementary school, and a library. Just off of the green was a strip of retail stores that included two of my favorites, a drugstore with a soda fountain counter and a hardware store. Many of my best times were spent in one of these two spots. On Saturdays, my mom would bring her three daughters to the drugstore counter for grilled cheese and milkshakes. I always got vanilla. This was a great outing; my mom always said it was a "blast from her past." But my favorite Saturdays were the ones when my grandfather, Papa, joined us.

As the youngest girl, I got to go next door to the hardware store after lunch with Papa. I'm not sure I even remember where my sisters went; all other reality vanished when I stepped through the doors into that magical world. Papa would usually have some reason for being there, some small part he needed, but I knew that he would spend quite a bit of the day chatting with the owner and other customers. He would have a soda and sit in the chair by the window. His friendliness gave me what I needed, the ability to roam and explore without concern for time. My love affair with hardware had begun.

At first I was just a voyeur; I would look for hours through the aisles, contemplating the use for various drill bits and sections of pipe. When the owner began to trust me, he would let me rummage freely, knowing I wouldn't mix up the 16-penny framing nails with the 8-penny finish nails. By the time I was nine, I spent less time randomly searching; I now had a clear purpose and knew what I wanted. My path was direct; I avoided the paint section and went straight for the buckets and bins. Countless small drawers slid open to reveal their mysteries: fancy wing nuts, brass clamps, sliding latches and a multitude of sizes of simple nuts and bolts. I didn't have to wonder about the uses for this hardware, I knew immediately what they were made for.

Necklaces of hex nuts and washers, strung on bits of twine or leather strapping, began to appear around my neck. I made bracelets for all my best friends, fashioning new creations from leftover bits that had long since lost their meaning. A pipe clamp became a ring, until my finger started to turn strange and frightening colors. I even made jewelry for my dog; the cat wasn't as patient. Soon my sisters began commissioning new work. I had found my destiny. I was an artist.

GETTING STARTED

CHAPTER

1

A VISIT TO
THE HARDWARE STORE

The classic hardware store is the embodiment of organized disarray. At first glance, it appears to have no structure, but on closer inspection, a clearly discernable hierarchy of organization emerges. Plumbing is separate from electrical, wire and cable have their own aisle with various types of ropes and string, and hand tools are distinct from power tools. The section of fasteners (nuts/bolts, screws, nails) could occupy a creative spirit for hours. There is also specialty hardware for doors, windows, and cabinets. Paint, garden supplies, and miscellaneous household goods often round out the inventory. Fishing tackle and boat hardware are also quite adaptable. Go spend an afternoon and see what inspires you.

Making Designer Jewelry from Hardware, Beads, and Gems

PIECES AND PARTS

The following are a few of my favorite supplies that I use on a regular basis. Most of the hardware featured can be categorized as fasteners, but a lot of hardware is adaptable to jewelry design.

A - Nuts

B - Washers

C - Ferrules and stops

D - Screws and threaded inserts

E - Chain

F - Pulley

G - Springs

H - Split Rings

I - Compression sleeves

J - Shackles and clips

K - Hooks and links

METAL 101: KNOW YOUR MATERIALS

Not all hardware is made of metal, but if you spend enough time in a hardware store you will begin to see the importance of knowing the different features and possible uses for metal. Your choice of metal will be influenced by additional elements in your piece, such as the color of gemstones or beads, and also will be dictated by the design. Some metal is easier to form, and some is more resistant to abrasion or corrosion. The following chart indicates the more pertinent features of metal for the jewelry projects in this book and shows the types of hardware for each metal that I regularly use in my designs.

MATERIAL	FEATURES	PROJECT USES
ALUMINUM	Lightweight, soft material, matte finish, corrosion resistant, silver color	ferrules, stops, nuts, washers
BRASS	Warm color, shiny surface, soft material, corrosion resistant, will dull without polishing, an alloy of copper and zinc	nuts, washers, compression sleeves, split rings, screws, inserts. pulleys, hooks, shackles, springs, links, clips, chain, wire
BRONZE	Warm color, harder than copper, abrasion and corrosion resistant, an alloy of copper and tin	nuts, washers
COPPER	Soft material that will show abrasion, rust resistant, acquires a green patina over time	ferrules, nuts, washers, sheet metal, tubing, wire
GOLD	Warm color, will not tarnish or corrode, soft material that will show abrasion	finish findings, wire
SILVER	Soft material that will show abrasion, shiny surface, will tarnish, but not corrode	finish findings, sheet metal, wire
STAINLESS STEEL	Excellent corrosion and abrasion resistance, will not tarnish or rust	nuts, washers, screws, inserts, pulleys, hooks, shackles, clips, springs, split rings, links, wire, chain

Note on metals not used in this book:

Some materials, such as galvanized steel and iron, have coatings that prevent rust or corrosion. Zinc, tin, and chromium are often used as coatings on ferrous metal. The coatings, if scratched or abraded over time, can cause the underlying metal to be exposed and leave your jewelry unprotected. Nickel is a hard material with a shiny surface and is highly resistant to corrosion. Stainless steel is used where nickel might be considered, it is more readily available, and its surface will not dull over time. Titanium and platinum are two of the most durable metals. Titanium has a very high strength-to-weight ratio, having the same strength of other metals at half the weight. Both titanium and platinum will not tarnish, abrade, or corrode. Titanium is visually similar to aluminum and not readily available. Platinum is also not used for projects in this book, but only because it is generally cost prohibitive.

Special Note: Do not use lead! It is highly malleable, but very toxic.

BASIC SUPPLIES

It is sometimes difficult to choose from the enormous quantity of jewelry-making materials available today. The selection available through the Internet alone can be overwhelming. Add to that catalogs, jewelry shows, and magazines and one might be ready to throw up one's hands. Buy the basics first and then start to see what direction your designs take you. Also, do not overlook your local craft and bead stores as they can be quite helpful in simplifying the process and can provide hands-on guidance in your projects. In the end, personal preference, cost, and availability will all play a role in deciding what supplies you have on hand.

A "finding" is the term used for the little incidentals required for completing a piece of jewelry. Findings used for the projects in this book are generally made of sterling silver, bronze, copper, or other base metals. There are a daunting variety of types available, but the Resources section (page 124) provides suggestions on where to purchase quality findings. There are also endless possibilities for stringing jewelry, and the choice will determine the overall look of the piece. Some materials are more modern than others and impart a more innovative feeling. The following findings and stringing materials are the necessary components for the projects in this book.

EAR HOOKS
Ear hooks are easy to make and are also available in a large variety of designs. French wire ear hooks and kidney hooks are used for the projects in this book.

EAR POSTS
Ear posts are the alternative to ear hooks; posts add a stylish finish to any pair of earrings. The ring attached to the post opens to allow an added element.

EAR HOOPS
There are many different styles and sizes of ear hoops, and there are an infinite number of designs that can be created around them.

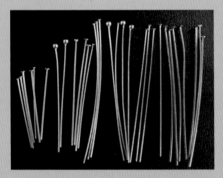

HEAD PINS

Head pins resemble an upside-down nail. They are made up of a straight piece of wire with a flat head on the end. Head pins are used to make earrings, dangles, or other components and come in a wide variety of lengths and diameters.

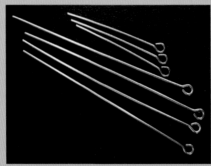

EYE PINS

Eye pins are similar to head pins but have a small loop, or eye, on one end. Eye pins are used to attach to chain, another eye pin, or to provide a loop for a dangle. They can also be used with a bead whose hole is too large for a head pin.

CRIMP BEADS

Crimp beads are small metal beads that are used to finish off necklaces and bracelets strung with stringing wire. They come in a tube shape or round bead; the tube shape is used in the projects in this book.

JUMP RINGS AND SPLIT RINGS

Jump rings are used frequently in jewelry making in conjunction with clasps or to form links. Split rings are also available in various sizes.

CORD END AND PINCH END CLASPS

Cord end caps are used with leather, rubber, fabric cord, or ribbon. Adjustable cord end clasps are another option if you need to allow for size differences. Smaller cord end caps are used for memory wire. Pinch end clasps are perfect for finishing off the ends of wider materials such as mesh tubing, ribbon, or rubber. They come in a variety of widths and are easy to use.

CLASPS

Clasps come in a variety of designs and materials. If you are not creating your own clasp, take some time to familiarize yourself with all the options. Many of the projects in this book use large lobster clasps, hook and eye clasps, and toggle clasps. This choice is one of the more important design decisions; it can significantly change the look of your piece.

CHAIN

Chain is used for several of the projects in this book. It is always popular and can be used in an amazing variety of ways. Chain is sold by the foot in different lengths, diameters, and patterns.

STRINGING WIRE

There are different brands of stringing wire on the market, including Soft Flex, Beadalon, and Accu-Flex. Depending on the manufacturer, there are various sizes and colors available. Beadalon is used in the projects in this book, in either 0.018" (0.46 mm) or 0.012" (0.30 mm) diameter. The 0.018" (0.46 mm) diameter is preferred for most designs as it is stronger and less likely to break; the holes drilled for some pearls or gemstones require the smaller-diameter stringing wire.

LEATHER

Leather cord has become quite popular with today's casual styles. It comes in an almost infinite range of colors and types. The highest quality cording comes from Greece, but round leather cording can be found easily in widths ranging from 1 mm to 4 mm. Woven or machine-braided cord adds a polished look and more design options.

RUBBER

Rubber is available in cord, tube, or flat sections and in a myriad of colors. Rubber tube can be combined with memory wire to take on unique shapes. The flat sections are perfect for cuff bracelets when combined with a pinch end clasp.

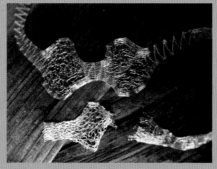

MESH TUBING

Mesh tubing is a stretchable material that is available in base metals or in silver and gold in widths ranging from approximately 6 mm to 20 mm. The sterling mesh is considerably more expensive than the base metal, but also comes in a range of enameled colors. Obviously, gold mesh is used for only the most important pieces.

FABRIC AND RIBBON

Waxed cotton, vinyl, and satin are three of the most popular options for fabric cording. Ribbon in varying widths and colors can be a dynamic contrast to the tougher look of hardware.

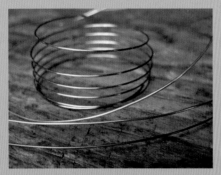

WIRE

Sterling silver, gold, brass, and copper wire are all readily available. Memory wire is a popular name for wire made from stainless steel. All wire can be wrapped or shaped to make unique designs and can be combined with other materials such as tubing.

SILK

Silk thread is traditionally used for knotting between pearls, but can be used in stringing other materials. You must be careful that your materials do not have sharp edges as they will fray the silk and eventually cause it to break. You can purchase silk on large spools or wrapped around cards with an attached needle. It comes in a variety of colors and is available in a range of sizes. Generally size "F" (0.0137" [0.348 mm]) is preferred.

FLEXIBLE NEEDLE

This is the needle you will use for stringing with silk. It has a large eye that collapses when threaded through the bead and is made of twisted wire.

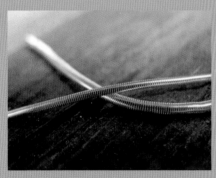

FRENCH WIRE

Used for completing a design strung on silk, French wire is a springlike coil of wire available in a silver or gold finish.

BASE METAL EXPANSION BAND

This band is used for one of the bracelet projects in the book. It provides an easy start for an infinite variety of possible designs. It is available in three-row or two-row styles with white or yellow finish.

THE TOOLBOX: JEWELRY-MAKING TOOLS

Vintage toolboxes have always been a source of inspiration for me. I store all of my high-tech jewelry-making tools in a series of wooden and metal boxes collected over the years. But while I use antique toolboxes for storage and often use old hardware from the local hardware store or even junk shop, I never use old tools in my jewelry making. In other words, feel free to clean up that old toolbox from your basement and rummage through piles of leftover hardware, but remember, leave the basement tools behind.

Many of the tools used for projects in this book might be similar to tools you have on hand, but jewelry-making tools are precision crafted. They provide a professional quality of finish to your designs. The tools you select now will affect your finished product later. While thirty dollars might seem a lot for a pair of pliers, keep in mind that if they are properly maintained, you will have them for a very long time. Nothing is more frustrating than investing your time, dollars, and effort only to ruin the finished product with an inferior set of tools.

Finally, instead of amassing a large quantity of tools, invest in a few important ones. Remember, a great deal of effort goes into designing a piece of jewelry. In fact, if each piece is unique, the amount of time you spend will probably be the most expensive component of your design. By choosing the highest quality materials and tools that you can find and finance, the finished work will be cherished for years.

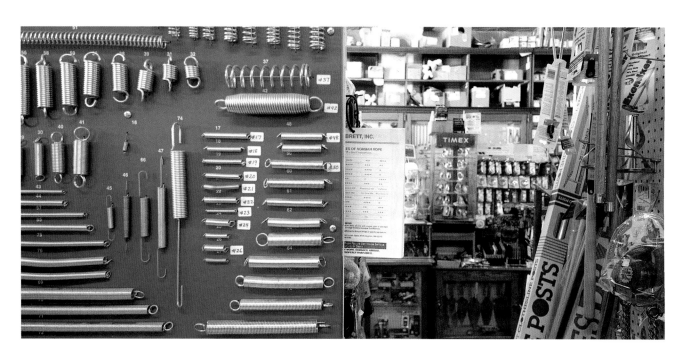

Beading Cloth

A variety of synthetic beading cloths are available. They are absolutely necessary in the design and creation of jewelry. Your surface must be clean and your materials must stay in place throughout the process. I prefer a beading cloth to a beading board, as it allows more creativity in the design process.

Flat-Nosed Pliers

For bending and gripping wire, flat-nosed pliers are necessary. Make sure you get a pair that is smooth and not textured on the inside of the nose; the texture will scratch your wire or metal.

Round-Nosed Pliers

If you plan to create any sort of curl or loop with wire, round-nosed pliers will need to be in your toolbox. These are designed specifically for jewelry making; you will not find them at your local hardware store. The tips of these pliers are cone shaped, which provide a smooth area for curling wire to create a variety of diameter loops.

Flush-Cut Wire Cutters

A high quality pair of flush-cut wire cutters is my favorite tool. A pair of jeweler-quality flush-cut wire cutters cut the wire at a 90-degree angle enabling the end of the wire to be flat and smooth. A good pair of flush-cut cutters will reduce the amount of filing necessary and will produce a professional piece of jewelry. To maintain the investment, these pliers should not be used for any other purpose.

Crimping Pliers

Crimp beads can only be correctly attached with a pair of crimping pliers. In fact, crimping pliers are designed just for this task. The black crimping pliers have two notches in the nose that are used to fold and then press the crimp bead closed.

Crimping Pliers

The blue-handled crimping pliers are a new patented design that allows for a smoother, seamless crimp.

Split Ring Pliers
(Not Shown)

These odd-looking pliers easily pry open a split jump ring, allowing you to slide on your charm, clasp, or whatever it is you are attaching. Once the attachment is into the ring, continue sliding the pliers around, pushing the charm along with your fingers until it dangles freely and securely.

Jeweler's Files

Even if you use a good pair of wire cutters, you will occasionally need to file the ends of wire smooth. Jeweler's files are made specifically for working with metal. The files normally come in a set of six to twelve files in different shapes (flat, round, square, and half-round) and grits. Keep them in the case they arrive in; otherwise, they have a way of being misplaced.

Reamers

A pearl reamer is the best tool for enlarging the holes in pearls. The diamond-tip reamer has three different tips that can be used to either smooth or enlarge holes in beads or gemstones.

Dremel or Flex-Shaft and Drill Bits (not shown)

This is an invaluable tool for anyone creating jewelry. Attachments can ream holes quickly in most materials or polish edges of sharp metals or stones. Buy a flex-shaft from a jewelry-making catalog, as the ones in hardware stores typically do not have fine enough tips or varied enough attachments. Most flex-shafts have foot pedals and can be mounted to your

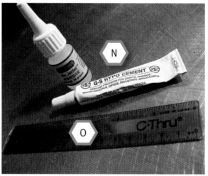

surface is adequate for most of my stamping needs and the hardwood pin is an essential surface for filing.

 ### LEATHER PUNCH

A high-quality leather punch is necessary when working with leather materials.

DRILL PRESS (NOT SHOWN)

This is the one tool I have stolen from my husband. It needed quite a dusting off, but with an additional chuck that can hold fine-gauge tips; his drill press has proven quite adequate. Sets of high-speed drill bits are available from jewelry-making catalogs. You can use a Dremel or flex-shaft as an alternative to the drill press; if you have a drill press, you will probably prefer this tool as the drilling will be faster and easier.

 ### JEWELER'S CEMENT

Many different manufacturers sell glue or cement for jewelry making. Different glues are necessary for different materials. For most stringing, you can use Hypo-Tube Cement, which has the slender tip at the end. An epoxy or fast-acting adhesive, such as Rio JetSet, is recommended for rubber and leather.

 ### RULER

A ruler is a simple tool, but necessary. You should have both standard and metric varieties in your toolbox; clear acrylic is useful.

---

workbench, allowing for increased maneuverability. The drill bits attach to the chuck in the flex-shaft and are much finer than the ones sold in hardware stores. Diamond head drill bits are preferred for drilling holes in pearls and gemstones.

 ### MANDREL

Tapered ring and stepped bracelet mandrels are used for forming wire. It creates a perfect curve without marking the wire or metal. Mandrels are attached to my workbench with a vise clamp.

 ### HAMMERS

Three hammers that you may use frequently are a 4-oz ball-peen hammer,

a rawhide mallet, and a large brass head mallet. The ball-peen hammer flattens or shapes wire depending on the side of the hammer used; one side is flat and the other is half-domed. The rawhide hammer will not mar the surface when forming metal.

 ### METAL STAMPS

There are many sets of metal stamps available. Simple small letters and numbers are an essential addition to your toolbox. Many other varieties of symbols are available (K).

 ### BENCH PIN AND ANVIL

A bench pin and anvil attaches to your work surface with a clamp. The metal

JEWELRY-MAKING TECHNIQUES

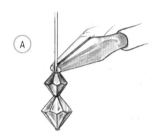

WRAP LOOP

The wrap loop technique is used for a wide variety of jewelry projects. It is extremely durable and attaches the elements of your design securely. This technique is used to make earrings, add dangles to necklaces or bracelets, or make connections between different components. Be patient and practice with scraps of wire. You will want to master this skill to make perfectly round wraps without any space between the end of your wrap and the pearl or bead it contains. For this technique, you will need round-nosed pliers, flat-nosed pliers, flush-cut wire cutters, a jeweler's file, and a head pin or wire to create wrap loops.

1. Start by using the flat-nosed pliers to bend the wire to a 90-degree angle so that you create an upside-down L shape (**A** and **B**).

2. Position the nose of your round-nosed pliers in the bend that you created in step 1 (**C**).

3. Use your fingers to wrap the wire around the nose of your pliers to form a loop (**D**).

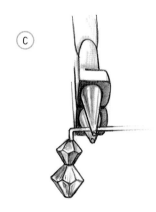

4. While you are keeping the round-nosed pliers inside the loop, hold the loop against the nose of the pliers with one finger (**E**). You should have your round-nosed pliers in one hand with one finger pressing the loop against the nose. (If you are right-handed, then you will probably want to use your left hand to hold the pliers and your pointer finger to hold the loop against the nose.)

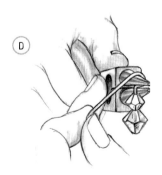

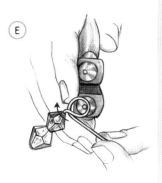

5. Using your other hand (if you are right-handed, the right hand), start to wrap the loose wire around the straight piece of wire that is directly under your loop. If the wire is soft, you can probably do this with your fingers. Otherwise, use flat-nosed pliers to hold the loose wire and wrap (**F**).

6. Continue to wrap as many times as you want, and, if necessary, trim off excess wire with wire cutters and file the ends smooth with a jeweler's file (**G**).

7. Use your flat-nosed pliers to press the wire-wrap end flat to make sure it does not scratch or poke.

8. If necessary, use your round-nosed pliers to straighten the loop.

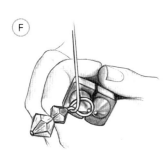

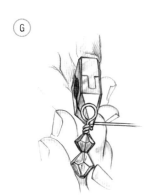

SIMPLE LOOP

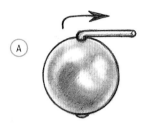

This technique is a simplified version of the wrap loop technique. Although wrapping the wire around itself is more secure, this simple loop technique can be surprisingly strong if done properly with a thick enough gauge of wire. For this procedure, you will need round-nosed pliers, flat-nosed pliers, flush-cut wire cutters, and a 22-gauge (0.65 mm) head pin or section of wire.

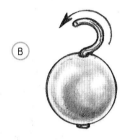

1. Use your flat-nosed pliers to bend the head pin to a 90-degree angle (**A**).

2. Make sure that the part of the head pin that is bent is about 1/2" (1.3 cm) long, and, if necessary, trim any excess with wire cutters.

3. Position the bent part of the head pin so that it is facing away from you.

4. Then, using round-nosed pliers, grasp the end of the bent head pin and make sure that the middle part of the pliers' nose is holding the pin. Do not allow any of the wire to protrude from the other end of the pliers. This will make the end of your loop complete the perfect circle. After positioning your pliers correctly, slowly curl the wire toward you (**B**).

5. Because the first curl will probably not complete the entire loop, release and reposition your pliers on the circle loop you have started.

6. Continue to curl it toward you until you have made a full circle (**C**).

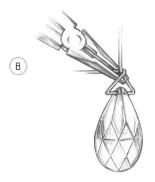

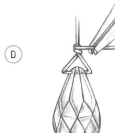

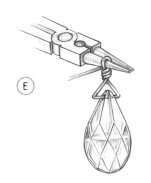

WRAP BAIL

The wrap bail is typically used when attaching a pendant to a chain or cord. The technique is a good one to master, as it can be adapted to a variety of projects. Practice on scrap wire until you get the technique perfected.

1. Cut a section of wire approximately 3" (7.6 cm) in length and file both ends smooth. The exact length will depend on the size of bead or element you are attaching as a bail.

2. Thread the wire one-third of the way through the bead and bend both sections of wire up around the bead. There are many ways to do this, depending on the look you want; either use flat-nosed pliers for a straight edge or use your fingers for a more natural look (**A**).

3. Using the flat-nosed pliers, bend the one-third length of wire so that it is perpendicular and sticking out toward the left of the bead (**B**).

4. Using the flat-nosed pliers, bend the two-thirds length of wire so that this section is perpendicular and sticking out toward the right of the bead (**C**).

5. Taking the longer section, bend the wire again, 45 degrees, so that the wire is pointing straight up and is directly over the center of the bead.

6. Holding this section of wire in the jaws of the flat-nosed pliers, wrap the other section of wire around the center wire twice, ending the wrap in what will become the back of the bail. Trim off the excess wire (**D**).

7. Using round-nosed pliers, create a standard wrap loop with the other section of wire, completing the bail so that the end is next to the other end of wire. Trim off any excess. Make sure you attach the bail to your design before completing the wrap, unless it hangs freely from a chain or cord (**E**).

FIGURE EIGHT

The figure eight is easily adapted to hook and eye clasps or connectors between design elements. Imagine it elongated or pinched closed on one end or two and you will begin to see the importance of this simple technique.

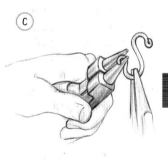

1. Cut a section of wire approximately 2" (5.1 cm) in length and file both ends smooth.

2. Positioning your round-nosed pliers slightly more than halfway on the wire, gently wrap the wire around the nose of the pliers with your nondominant hand. The wire should be wrapped around the thicker part of the nose of the pliers to create a gentle curve (**A**).

3. Repeat step 2 on the other side of the wire so that the curve is facing the other direction (**B**).

4. Using round-nosed pliers, create small curls on both ends of the wire (**C**).

JEWELER'S FILES

When cutting wire to create jewelry components such as dangles or earrings, you may notice that the ends of your wire may be rough to the touch. These rough spots can poke or scratch and catch on clothing. A professional designer uses a jeweler's file to smooth the ends.

1. After cutting a piece of wire, run the file in one direction against the end that was cut. Always file in one direction, never back and forth.

2. After making a piece of jewelry that uses wire, use your fingers to double-check the wire areas (such as wrap loops, for example) to ensure that the wire is smooth. If you feel a rough spot, run the file in one direction against this area again.

CRIMP BEADS

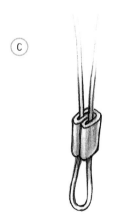

A piece of jewelry can be finished on the ends in a number of different ways. I prefer the look of stringing wire and crimp beads to nylon thread and bead tips, but it is really a matter of personal preference. Many of the projects in this book use stringing wire and crimp beads, but nylon thread and bead tips can be substituted for some of them. To use crimp beads, a pair of crimping pliers is required. In addition to crimping pliers, you will need tube-shaped crimp beads, round-nosed pliers, flush-cut wire cutters, and beading wire.

1. Slide one crimp bead onto the end of a piece of beading wire and loop the wire back through the crimp bead after adding the clasp or other jewelry component such as a section of chain or a wrapped element (**A**).

2. Position the crimp bead inside the second notch in the crimping pliers (the one closest to you when you are holding the pliers in your hand), making sure that the wire has not twisted inside the crimp bead. Close the pliers firmly around the crimp bead. You should see the crimp bead now has a groove down the middle so that it curls (**B**).

3. Now, position the same crimp bead in the first notch in the pliers, aligning the groove with the opening of the crimping pliers. Close the pliers very tightly around the initial crimp so that you are flattening the curl (**C**).

4. Use wire cutters to trim off all but about 1/4" (6 mm) of excess beading wire.

5. Add your pearls, making sure you slide the first pearl over both pieces of wire on the end. It is quite possible that the stringing wire will not pass through the hole in the pearls a second time. You have the choice of reaming the pearls to allow this second pass or cutting the wire flush with the end of the crimp bead. If you have crimped the bead securely, cutting it flush will not be a problem.

6. Once you have completed the stringing of your design, you are ready to finish the other end. Slide a second crimp bead onto the end of your wire.

7. After adding the clasp or other jewelry component, loop the wire back through the crimp bead, making sure it does not twist within the crimp bead, and thread the stringing wire back though the last pearl on this end of the wire.

8. Insert the nose of your round-nosed pliers into the loop.

9. While holding your round-nosed pliers with one hand, gently pull the beading wire with your other hand so that you push the crimp bead up against the other beads. This will ensure that you do not have any extra slack in your beaded piece and that you also keep the end loop of your beading wire intact.

10. Repeat steps 2 and 3 to close the crimp bead.

11. Finish by using wire cutters to trim off the excess beading wire.

Freshwater pearls and stones are often drilled with holes too small to allow for thicker-gauge wire or for double passes of stringing wire or silk. Since pearls are a relatively soft material, it is easy to hand-ream a larger hole. An electric Dremel or diamond-edged reamer is necessary for harder materials. There are a wide variety of Dremels and flex-shafts on the market; many have foot pedals and can be mounted directly to your workbench to allow for more maneuverability.

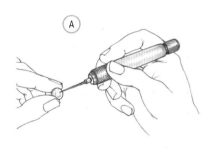

HAND REAMING:

1. Hold the pearl in one hand while gently passing the pearl reamer back and forth through one side of the hole of the pearl. Let the reamer do the work; using too much force will break the tip of the reamer. You should notice a cloud of white powder coming from inside the pearl and each pass should feel smoother and allow the reamer to enter the pearl further (**A**).

2. Turn the pearl over and insert the reamer in the opposite direction.

3. Repeat step 1 until the reamer passes completely through the pearl.

ELECTRIC DREMEL OR FLEX-SHAFT:

1. Using the proper diamond drill bit for the size hole you desire, immerse the stone, glass, or ceramic bead in a water bath and position the Dremel so that only the tip of the Dremel will be submerged while drilling. The water bath is necessary if you are not using a lubricant when drilling to protect the diamond head of the drill bit and to allow for effective drilling.

2. Hold the stone or bead in your free hand or in a vise clamp while your other hand gently applies pressure to the bead with the Dremel. Do not force the Dremel; this will only result in broken drill bits. Have patience and let the diamond-head tip do the work (**A**).

DRILLING METAL

To drill metal, I use a drill press with a chuck that can accommodate fine jewelry drill bits. Make sure you use eye protectors when operating this piece of equipment. You can substitute a Dremel or flex-shaft for projects that specify a drill press, though if you have a drill press, you will find the drill press faster and easier.

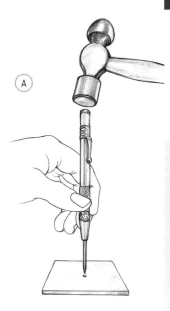

1. Using a center punch, mark the exact location of the hole that is desired. A short tap is all that is needed; too strong a tap will bend the metal. This shallow dimple not only marks the location, but also provides a guide for the drill bit-making it less likely that the metal will slide (**A**).

2. Once you have the location, align the center of your bit to the mark on the metal. It is helpful to have a clip on the drill press that secures the metal, but you will need to use your hands to make sure that the metal does not move as the drilling commences (**B**).

3. Using a slow speed, allow the drill bit to pierce the metal. A lubricant, such as beeswax, is a good idea to protect the fine edges of the drill bit.

4. Finally, use a polisher to remove any metal shavings.

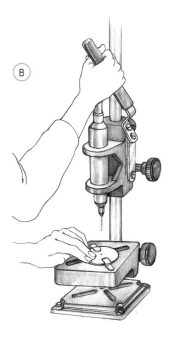

BENDING WIRE OR METAL

Wire is easily bent with a pair of smooth-sided round-nosed pliers. A mandrel is useful if you want a large bend in the wire or metal. There are also a wide variety of forming pliers with different jaws to make the process easier; your selection depends on how much use you will get from the tool and the depth of your pocketbook.

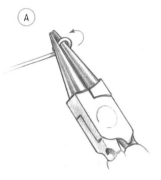

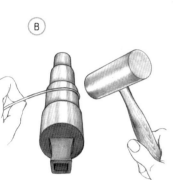

1. Select the size of the pliers depending on the size of the bend you desire and guide the wire around the bend with your free hand (**A**).

2. Alternatively, attach a mandrel to a bench pin and use your free hand and a rubber mallet to form the wire around the mandrel. The rubber mallet will prevent the metal from being marred (**B**).

LEATHER PUNCH

There are a variety of hole punches that can be used in jewelry making. Leather punches, metal punches, and grommet punches are all handy to have in your toolbox. The technique is the same no matter which one you use.

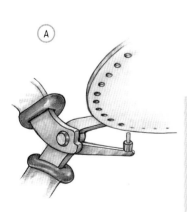

1. Mark the location of the hole you desire with a pencil or marker depending on the material you are piercing.

2. Turn the punch so that the hole is facing upwards and you can see the mark through the hole of the punch (**A**).

3. With a smooth action, squeeze the punch, creating a hole as desired.

STAMPING

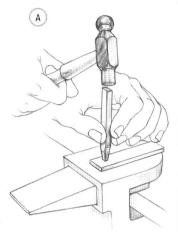

Stamping metal is easy and creative and gives an individual touch to your work. There are many metal stamp sets to choose from; letters, numbers, and symbols are all readily available in an array of sizes.

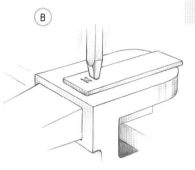

1. Position the piece of metal that will accept the stamp on the flat metal surface of a bench pin.

2. Select the first stamp and hold it in your nondominant hand with the symbol resting on the metal in the exact location you desire.

3. Firmly hammer the stamp in a fluid motion with a ball-peen hammer. Do not tap lightly or tap the hammer more than once. It is possible to restamp the metal if the impression is not clear, but it is a risky business, and it is quite likely that you will end up with a blurred image (**A**).

4. Select the next stamp and align it parallel with the previous stamp. This will take some practice, but your eye is the best guide when working with small metal stamps. It is possible to draw a fine guideline with a pencil if you prefer (**B**).

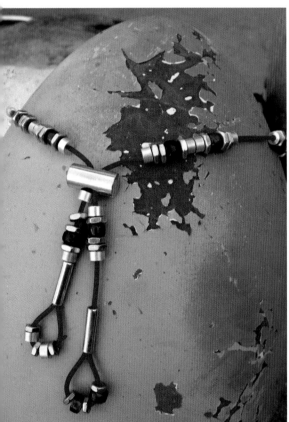

A FEW DAYS BEFORE CHRISTMAS IN 1914, EDWARD ENOCH NICHOLS AND PAUL AMBROSE WARNER OPENED THE DOORS OF NICHOLS HARDWARE IN PURCELLVILLE, VIRGINIA. IT IS THE OLDEST RETAIL BUSINESS STILL OWNED BY THE SAME FAMILY IN THE VIRGINIA PIEDMONT. WHEN YOU WALK INTO THE STORE, YOU IMMEDIATELY KNOW YOU ARE SOMEWHERE SPECIAL. ORIGINAL TIN CEILINGS MARK THE LONG HISTORY OF THE BUILDING, BUT IT IS THE FULL WALL OF WOODEN DRAWERS ON ONE SIDE OF THE STORE THAT TRULY IS AMAZING. EACH DRAWER HAS HARDWARE MOUNTED ON THE EXTERIOR INDICATING WHAT IS TO BE FOUND INSIDE. I HAVE ATTENDED OPENINGS FOR ART INSTALLATIONS THAT WERE ONLY HALF AS ENGAGING. THE HAPHAZARD DISPLAY IS UNIFIED BY THE WOODEN WALL AND THE END RESULT IS SIMPLY GORGEOUS. THEY HAVE EVERYTHING YOU COULD POSSIBLY NEED; IN FACT, THEIR MOTTO IS: "IF WE DON'T HAVE IT, YOU DON'T NEED IT." IN THE TRUE FAMILY TRADITION, ALL RECEIPTS ARE HANDWRITTEN AND THEY ARE OPEN SEVEN DAYS A WEEK. TED NICHOLS WAS NICE ENOUGH TO SHOW ME AROUND AND I WAS LUCKY ENOUGH TO FIND A FEW NEW ODDS AND ENDS THAT INSPIRED ME.

NECKLACES

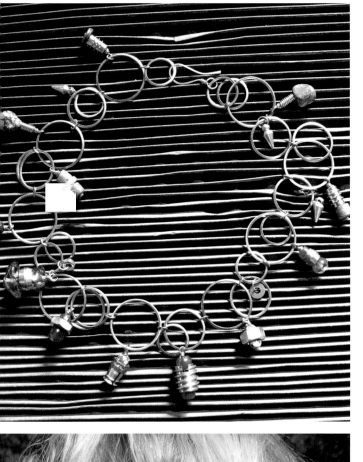

WIGGLY WASHERS

This necklace uses stainless steel flat washers as the focal point of the design and as part of the clasp. The round shapes of the freshwater pearls and the multicolored foil glass beads complement the disk shape of the washers. Four different sizes of washers are alternated in a symmetrical pattern, adding rhythm and movement to the necklace. The silver in the foil beads sparkle and work well with the silverlike finish of the stainless steel. The clasp is not only simple and innovative, but also provides secure closure.

MATERIALS

THIRTY-SIX SMALL 12 MM STAINLESS STEEL FLAT WASHERS

EIGHT MEDIUM 16 MM STAINLESS STEEL FLAT WASHERS

THREE LARGE 18 MM STAINLESS STEEL FLAT WASHERS

SIXTEEN 6 MM WHITE POTATO PEARLS

FORTY 8 MM CZECH FOIL GLASS BEADS

ONE 7/8" (2.2 CM) ROUND SWIRL PAPER CLIP

TWO 2 MM STERLING SILVER CRIMP BEADS

20" (50.8 CM) NYLON-COATED STAINLESS STEEL STRINGING WIRE BEADALON 49 STRAND: 0.018" (0.46 MM) DIAMETER

FLUSH-CUT WIRE CUTTERS

CRIMPING PLIERS

1. Start by stringing one sterling silver crimp bead onto the Beadalon wire.

2. Add the repeating pattern: pearl, foil bead, small 12 mm washer, foil bead, pearl.

3. Add the following: foil bead, small 12 mm washer, foil bead, small 12 mm washer, medium 16-mm washer, small 12 mm washer, foil bead, small 12 mm washer, foil bead.

4. Add the repeating pattern: pearl, foil bead, small 12 mm washer, foil bead, pearl.

5. Add the following: small 12 mm washer, foil bead, small 12 mm washer, medium 16 mm washer, small 12 mm washer, foil bead, small 12 mm washer.

6. Add the repeating pattern: pearl, foil bead, small 12 mm washer, foil bead, pearl.

7. Add the following: foil bead, small 12 mm washer, foil bead, small 12 mm washer, medium 16 mm washer, small 12 mm washer, foil bead, small 12 mm washer, foil bead (same as step 3).

8. Add the repeating pattern: pearl, foil bead, small 12 mm washer, foil bead, pearl.

9. For the center pattern, add the following: foil bead, small 12 mm washer, foil bead, small 12 mm washer, medium 16 mm washer, large 18 mm washer, medium 16 mm washer, small 12 mm washer, foil bead, small 12 mm washer, foil bead.

10. Continue stringing the hardware, beads, and pearls using the reverse patterns to complete a symmetrical necklace.

11. Add the final sterling silver crimp bead.

12. Slip one of the large 18 mm washers onto the end of the Beadalon. Pass the Beadalon back through the crimp and **crimp** to close.

13. Repeat for the other end.

14. Thread the round wavy paper clip all the way through one of the end washers until completely attached.

15. To clasp, thread the paper clip halfway onto the other washer. For a more secure closure, thread all the way onto the paper clip. Threading both sides all the way on does make it completely secure, but it also makes it harder to get on and off; I have found that halfway is adequate.

JEWELER'S TIP

Over the years, I have made many of the clasps for my Softhardwear designs. Hex nuts are an obvious choice, but much of the hardware in this book can be adapted to clasps and closures. Miniature toggles and shanks are an innovative way to finish off a piece. Make sure whatever you choose, you construct it with the same care and professional attention you use for all your jewelry. Just because it is hardware doesn't mean the clasp shouldn't get the same attention as the rest of the design. In fact, it can be considered to be a focal point itself.

WOVEN RUBBER GASKETS

The patterns that are created from the round rubber gaskets and the ends of the leather cord resemble an industrial version of fine lace. Woven together, they form a mesh that is both interesting and accessible at the same time. The large brass linchpin echoes the geometries of the gaskets and is a creative way to clasp necklaces that end in large loops.

MATERIALS

THIRTY-SEVEN BLACK AND RED RUBBER GASKETS IN VARYING DIMENSIONS 1/2" TO 1 3/4"

TWO 20 MM BRASS FLAT WASHERS

THREE 18 MM BRASS FLAT WASHERS

ONE 2.5 CM WHITE PVC PLASTIC FLAT WASHER

ONE LARGE 5/16" (8 MM) BRASS LINCHPIN: 4.5-CM DIAMETER

15 3/4' (480 CM) LENGTH OF 1.5-MM BLACK GREEK LEATHER CORD

6" (15.2 CM) LENGTH OF 1.5-MM BLACK GREEK LEATHER CORD

FLUSH-CUT WIRE CUTTERS

PRECISION SCISSORS

1. Start by cutting the leather cord into fifty-four 3 1/2" (8.9 cm) sections. Set aside.

2. On a beading cloth, arrange the rubber gaskets in an arc, varying the diameters and colors of the rubber gaskets. Both ends of the arc should end with five of the small black rubber gaskets.

3. To this design, add the brass washers and the plastic washer, equally spacing, approximately 1 1/2" (3.8 cm) apart.

4. Starting at one end, firmly tie a clove hitch knot with a section of black leather cord, joining two gaskets together.

5. Work your way around the necklace, carefully maintaining the arc shape until all the gaskets and washers have been joined with the leather cord.

6. Using scissors, snip the ends of the leather cord evenly, allowing ends of approximately 3/4" (1.9 cm).

7. Using the 6" (15.2 cm) section of leather cord, tie two bowline knots onto the last rubber gasket on one side of the necklace, allowing a completed loop of 3/4" (1.9 cm) diameter. Trim off the excess leather cord, leaving ends of approximately 3/4" (1.9 cm). Guide the free end of the linchpin through the completed loop.

8. To clasp, simply guide the free end of the linchpin through the last rubber gasket on the opposite side of the necklace.

JEWELER'S TIP

Invest in a good book on knots; a properly tied knot is a handy trick to master. *The Ashley Book of Knots* is the bible for sailors and knot lovers alike, with 620 pages of illustrated and indexed knots. Instructional diagrams are also easy to find online. This design uses a clove hitch and a bowline knot, but many knots are easily adapted for jewelry design.

BRASS CHOKER

The warmth of brass works well with many different gemstones and pearls and there is a wide variety of brass hardware available. This necklace uses five different types of hardware. Each piece is distinctive enough to attract attention, but it is important that they also complement each other. The threaded inserts and the spring coils echo the ridges along the edges of the knurled nuts. The miniature plumb bobs break up the rhythm and bring the eye to the center. Finally, the larger hex nuts provide a good anchor for the figure-eight clasp.

1. String elements, alternating the hardware, pearls, turquoise, and beads. While it may not seem like there is a pattern, there are patterns within the symmetrical design.

2. Start by stringing one gold crimp bead.

3. Add the following pattern: pearl, bead, pearl, brass coil spring, pearl, bead, pearl, bead. Add a turquoise disk.

4. Add the following: bead, pearl, bead, pearl, small knurled nut, pearl, bead. Add a turquoise disk.

5. Add the following: bead, pearl, small hex nut, pearl, bead. Add a turquoise disk.

6. Add the following: bead, pearl, brass threaded insert, pearl, bead. Add a turquoise disk.

7. Add the following: bead, pearl, bead, pearl, large knurled nut, pearl, bead, pearl, bead. Add a turquoise disk.

8. Add the following: bead, pearl, bead, pearl, miniature plumb bob, pearl, bead, pearl, large knurled nut, pearl, bead, pearl, bead. Add the center turquoise disk.

9. Repeat the alternating pattern in the reverse order to create a symmetrical necklace. Add the final gold crimp bead.

10. Slip one of the large hex nuts onto the end of the Beadalon. Pass the Beadalon back through the crimp and **crimp** to close.

11. Repeat for the other end.

12. Create a **figure eight** from the 2" (5.1 cm) section of 14 kt gold wire and attach to one of the end hex nuts, closing one of the loops firmly.

13. To clasp, leave the other end of the figure eight open to slide on and off of the other hex nut.

MATERIALS

- TWO 6 MM BRASS HEX NUTS
- TWO 8 MM BRASS HEX NUTS
- TWO BRASS THREADED INSERTS
- TWO 8 MM BRASS COIL SPRINGS
- TWO 6 32 BRASS KNURLED NUTS
- FOUR 8-32 BRASS KNURLED NUTS
- TWO 13 MM BRASS PLUMB BOBS
- THIRTY-EIGHT 1 MM BRASS BEADS
- FORTY-THREE 4 MM WHITE POTATO PEARLS
- ELEVEN TURQUOISE DISKS
- 2" (5.1 CM) SECTION OF 14 KT GOLD 20-GAUGE (0.8 MM) WIRE
- TWO 2 MM 14 KT GOLD CRIMP BEADS
- 20" (50.8 CM) NYLON-COATED STAINLESS STEEL STRINGING WIRE BEADALON 49 STRAND: 0.018" (0.46 MM) DIAMETER
- FLUSH-CUT WIRE CUTTERS
- ROUND-NOSED PLIERS
- FLAT-NOSED PLIERS
- CRIMPING PLIERS

JEWELER'S TIP

THE TEMPTATION IS ALWAYS THERE TO ADD MORE TO A PIECE OF JEWELRY. THERE ARE SO MANY DIFFERENT BEADS AND GEMS NOW AVAILABLE TO THE JEWELRY DESIGNER; IF YOU ADD TO THIS VARIETY THE INFINITE ASSORTMENT OF HARDWARE, ONE CAN END UP WITH A MESS. MY STEPFATHER, AN ARTIST, ONCE TOLD ME THAT THE HARDEST PART OF PAINTING IS KNOWING WHEN YOU ARE DONE. THIS IS TRUE IN ALL DESIGN. THE MATERIALS CHOSEN SHOULD COMPLEMENT EACH OTHER OR CONTRAST IN AN UNUSUAL WAY. WHEN YOU ARE STARTING TO DESIGN, MAKE SURE THERE ARE NOT TOO MANY CONTRASTS AND THAT YOU HAVE A UNIFYING CONCEPT. TAKE A STEP BACK AND SEE IF YOUR EYE CAN ABSORB ALL YOU HAVE CREATED. THE POSSIBILITIES ARE ENDLESS, BUT IT IS IMPORTANT TO KNOW WHEN YOU ARE DONE.

LEATHER, BRASS, AND BRONZE

Leather cording is often used in Southwestern jewelry; I associate it with all the lariats I saw when I lived in Texas. While some of these pieces were quite elaborate and worn to the most posh gatherings, I usually think of leather cording for casual necklaces or bracelets. The warm colors of brass and bronze complement the coloring of the chocolate brown leather in this braided necklace. The small heavy brass pulley is the accent point; I found this one in a marine hardware store. Finally, the brass cabinet latch was stolen from my father-in-law's basement, from a wooden box he never got around to completing.

MATERIALS

TWELVE 9 MM BRONZE HEX NUTS

SIX 14 MM BRASS FLAT WASHERS

SIX 11 MM BRASS FLAT WASHERS

EIGHT 8- X 8 MM BRASS COMPRESSION RINGS

TWO 10 MM EZ-LOK THREADED INSERTS

ONE 1/4" x 3/4" (6 MM X 1.9 CM) BRASS PULLEY

ONE 1 1/2" (3.8 CM) BRASS CABINET LATCH

6" (15.2 CM) LENGTH OF 21-GAUGE (0.7 MM) BRASS WIRE

19" (48.3 CM) LENGTH OF FOUR-PLY BRAIDED BROWN LEATHER CORD

FLUSH-CUT WIRE CUTTERS

ROUND-NOSED PLIERS

FLAT-NOSED PLIERS

RIO JETSET ADHESIVE

1. Start by cutting the ends of the braided leather on a bias to make the threading easier. You should have an extra 1" (2.5 cm) length on each side, which you will trim off before finishing.

2. Thread on the pulley and guide it to the center of the leather cord. It should be tight enough on the leather to maintain its position.

3. Onto one side add a bronze hex nut, leaving a gap of 1/4" (6 mm) between it and the pulley. Follow by adding a compression ring, a 14 mm washer, and another compression ring.

4. Add three bronze hex nuts, spacing them 1/4" (6 mm) apart. Follow by adding a compression ring, an 11 mm washer, and another compression ring.

5. Add one bronze hex nut, leaving enough space for the compression rings and washers to move freely. Follow by adding a compression ring, a 14 mm washer, and another compression ring.

6. Add one bronze hex nut, again leaving enough space for the compression rings and washers to move freely. Follow by adding a compression ring, an 11 mm washer, a 14 mm washer, an 11 mm washer, and another compression ring.

7. Add the final bronze hex nut for this side of the necklace, again leaving enough space for the compression rings and washers to move freely.

8. Repeat steps 3–7 on the other side for a symmetrical necklace.

9. Cut the brass wire in half.

10. Thread one segment through the threaded insert, leaving 1" (2.5 cm) extending from the smaller diameter end of the threaded insert.

11. Make a large **wrap loop,** completing the wrap and cutting off any excess. The loop should be approximately 5 mm in diameter to allow for the cabinet latch.

12. Pull the brass wire so that the loop sits just above the threaded insert and the wrap is hidden.

13. Trim 1" (2.5 cm) from one end of the leather cord, apply adhesive to the end, and insert into the other end of the threaded insert.

14. Wrap the remainder of the brass wire around the threaded insert. Cut off any excess flush with the insert.

15. Repeat steps 10–14 on the other side, remembering to add the cabinet latch before you complete the **wrap loop.**

16. Properly measured and trimmed, this necklace should be 18" (45.7 cm) long.

JEWELER'S TIP

THE BRAIDED LEATHER SHOULD FIT SNUGGLY INSIDE THE THREADED INSERT. IF IT IS DIFFICULT TO PASS ENOUGH OF THE LEATHER CORD INTO THE INSERT, TRY TWISTING IT AS YOU INSERT OR USE THE TIP OF A PAIR OF FLAT-NOSED PLIERS OR A PAIR OF TWEEZERS TO GENTLY GUIDE IT IN. THE ADHESIVE IS VERY STRONG, BUT MAKE SURE YOU HAVE ENOUGH CONTACT BETWEEN THE LEATHER AND THE HARDWARE TO MAINTAIN A LASTING BOND.

COPPER RINGS

This necklace reminds me of a large charm bracelet with its oversized links and dangle embellishments. The copper rings are from a jewelry-making catalog, but copper fittings in the plumbing section are possible alternatives. Sometimes a fitting or fastener is inspiring in the hardware store, but the jewelry component is an easier or more available option. No matter which one is selected, the look is pure hardware, and the added embellishments make this a unique piece of art.

1. Using the 5 mm copper jump rings, link together the copper rings to make a chain, duplicating the following pattern three times: 1.6 cm, 2.5 cm, 2.1 cm, 2.5 cm, 2.1 cm, 2.5 cm.

2. Finish the chain with a small 1.6 cm ring.

3. Starting with the first jump ring link, add a small 1.6 cm ring. This will hang free from the link.

4. Skipping a link of the chain, at the third jump ring, add a medium 2.1 cm ring.

5. Continue in this alternating pattern of small and medium rings, adding a free-hanging ring to every other jump ring.

6. Hang the three miniature brass plumb bobs from separate 6 mm brass rings on the third copper rings from both ends and on the fifth copper ring from one end (do not count the free-hanging copper rings when determining where to attach the embellishments).

MATERIALS

NINE 1.6 CM COPPER RINGS

TEN 2.1 CM COPPER RINGS

NINE 2.5 CM COPPER RINGS

EIGHTEEN 5 MM COPPER JUMP RINGS

FIVE 6 MM BRASS JUMP RINGS

TWELVE 21-GAUGE (0.7 MM) 2" (5.1 CM) BRASS HEAD PINS

3" (7.6 CM) 21-GAUGE (0.7 MM) BRASS WIRE

BALL-PEEN HAMMER

FLUSH-CUT WIRE CUTTERS

ROUND-NOSED PLIERS

FLAT-NOSED PLIERS

ASSORTED HARDWARE AND GEMSTONE EMBELLISHMENTS:

ONE 8 MM COPPER FLAT WASHER

ONE 13 MM THREADED BRASS INSERT

ONE 9 MM BRASS COMPRESSION SLEEVE

ONE 15 MM BRASS COMPRESSION SLEEVE

ONE 12 MM BRASS EXPANSION SLEEVE

ONE 6 MM BRASS HEX NUT

THREE 11 MM BRASS HEX NUTS

TWO 10 MM EZ-LOK THREADED INSERTS

TWO 8 MM BRASS SPRING COILS

THREE 13 MM BRASS PLUMB BOBS

ONE 9 MM BLUE ANTIQUE TRADE BEAD DISK

TWO 10 MM TURQUOISE NUGGETS

THREE 7 MM ANTIQUE CARNELIAN BEADS

TWO 8 MM ROUND CARNELIAN BEADS

TWO 14- X 20 MM AMBER NUGGETS

THREE 6 MM CORAL ROUNDELS

SIX 6 MM ROUND JASPER BEADS

7. Counting from this same end, hang the 8 mm copper washer from a 6 mm brass ring on the seventh copper ring.

8. Counting from this same end, hang the 6 mm brass hex nut from a 6 mm brass ring on the thirteenth copper ring.

9. All of the remaining embellishments are attached to the copper rings with **wrap loops** using the 2" (5.1 cm) brass head pins. Assemble them in the following manner and order: turquoise nugget with brass spring coil, coral roundel with EZ-LOK threaded insert, carnelian round bead with 9-mm compression sleeve and antique carnelian bead, jasper bead with 11-mm brass hex nut and another jasper bead, antique carnelian bead with 13-mm threaded insert and another antique carnelian bead, expansion sleeve with jasper bead, carnelian round with 11-mm brass hex nut and jasper bead, amber nugget with 15-mm compression sleeve and amber nugget, jasper bead with 11-mm brass hex nut and another jasper bead, turquoise nugget with brass spring coil, blue antique trade bead disk with EZ-LOK threaded insert.

10. Skipping the two end 1.6-cm copper rings, attach the embellishments in the above order to separate copper rings, avoiding those rings that already have an embellishment attached. Complete the **wrap loops**.

11. From the 3" (7.6 cm) length of brass wire, fashion a hook clasp, adapting the **figure eight** technique to have a **wrap loop** closure on one end. Hammer the wire hook flat, work-hardening the material for additional stiffness.

JEWELER'S TIP

The additional step of adding free-hanging rings can easily be deleted. However, adding this design element brings movement and interest to what would be otherwise a simple chain of copper rings. Simplicity is sometimes sought after in design, but more complicated design can also be desirable. Knowing which is appropriate is the trick.

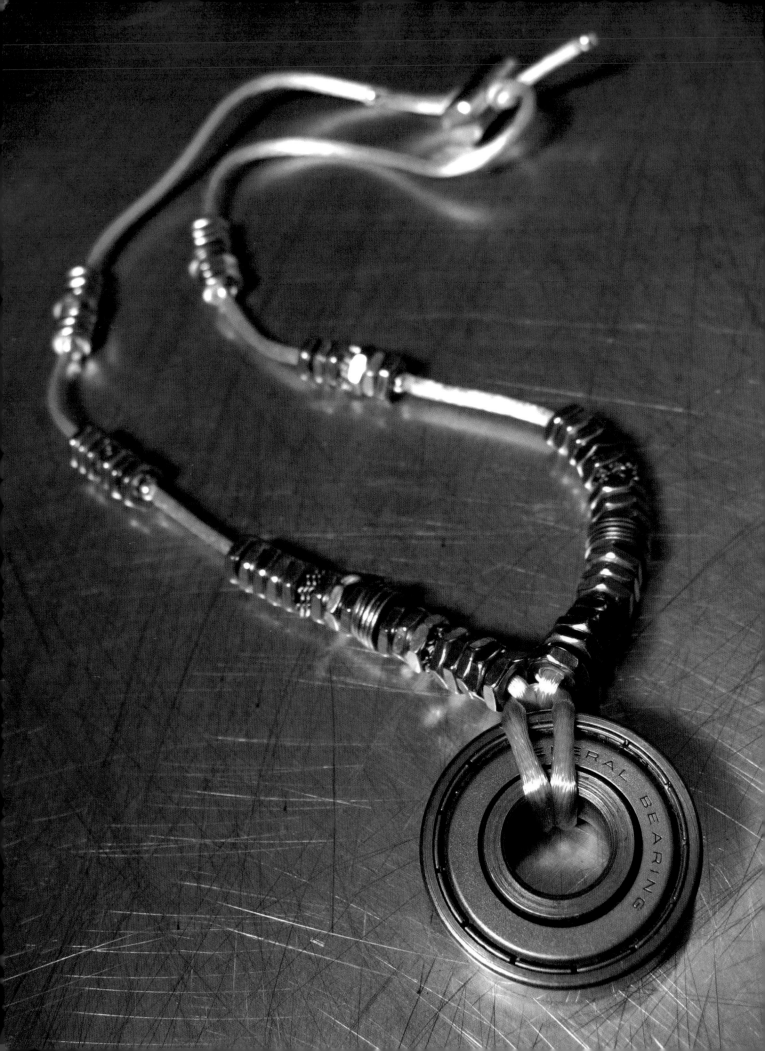

SATIN AND METAL

An interesting piece of hardware can serve as the focus for a design, dictating how the design will evolve. A large stainless steel ball-bearing ring used primarily with wheels and in small machinery is easily hung on satin cord using a lanyard hitch. The light pink satin cord contrasts with the heft of the metal fasteners. The necklace is finished with simple overhand knots that slide for adjustability.

FIFTY-SIX 8 MM STAINLESS STEEL HEX NUTS

EIGHTEEN 8 MM STAINLESS STEEL LOCK WASHERS

SIXTEEN 10 MM STAINLESS STEEL FLAT WASHERS

ONE 1 3/8" (3.5 CM) DIAMETER STAINLESS STEEL BALL-BEARING RING

ONE 3/4" x 3/8" (1.9 x 1 CM) ALUMINUM CROSS DOWEL JOINT CONNECTOR

SIX 2 MM STERLING SILVER CRIMP CAPS

36" (91.4 CM) LENGTH OF 2 MM PINK SATIN CORD

FLAT-NOSED PLIERS

1. Start by creating a lanyard hitch to attach the ball-bearing hardware to the center of the satin cord.

2. String the pattern onto the satin cord in the following order: five hex nuts, three lock washers, three hex nuts, five flat washers, three hex nuts, three lock washers, five hex nuts.

3. At 3 1/2" (8.9 cm) above the center of the necklace, add a sterling silver crimp cap and **crimp** tightly to the satin cord. This crimp will allow a 1" (2.5 cm) length of satin cord to show before the next section of hardware is added.

4. String the next pattern onto the satin cord in the following order: three hex nuts, three lock washers, three hex nuts.

5. At 5" (12.7 cm) above the center of the necklace, add a sterling silver crimp cap and **crimp** tightly to the satin cord. This crimp will allow another 1" (2.5 cm) length of satin cord to show before the next section of hardware is added.

6. String the next pattern onto the satin cord in the following order: three hex nuts, three flat washers, three hex nuts.

7. Repeat steps 2–6 on the other side of the cord to make a symmetrical necklace.

8. Thread both ends of the satin cord through the center hole of the cross dowel joint connector.

9. Tie overhand adjustable knots on each end.

10. Finish off both ends of the satin cord with crimp caps and **crimp** tightly to prevent fraying.

JEWELER'S TIP

Crimp caps and small metal beads can be used to space hardware or beads on cording or metal wire. They are essential when the design demands that the strung elements do not rest together. Use flat-nosed or round-nosed pliers depending on the crimp you are making, or use the specialty crimping pliers if a tight fit is possible and desirable.

NIOBIUM WIRE

This necklace uses a wire I had never heard of, niobium. Interestingly, it is a strong alloying element used in jet engine applications and rocket assemblies. It is also available to the jeweler. The best part is that it comes in a fantastic array of colors. A jagged assembly of assorted cotter pins projects a native or tribal feeling. The addition of spacing white freshwater pearls along the wire adds a geometric rhythm.

MATERIALS

THREE 2" (5.1 CM) HEAVY-GAUGE COTTER PINS

SIX 1" (2.5 CM) HEAVY-GAUGE COTTER PINS

SIX 1" (2.5 CM) LIGHT-GAUGE COTTER PINS

FOUR 3/4" (1.9 CM) LIGHT-GAUGE COTTER PINS

TWELVE 4 X 6 MM ALUMINUM STOPS

FOUR 10 MM WHITE COIN PEARLS

TWO 10 MM WHITE SQUARE PEARLS

EIGHT 6 MM ROUND PEARLS

TEN 1.8 MM STERLING SILVER ROUND CRIMP BEADS

TWO 0.025" (0.6 MM) STERLING SILVER END CAPS FOR MEMORY WIRE

TWO 6 MM STERLING SILVER JUMP RINGS

ONE 9 X 11 MM STERLING SILVER PUSH AND GRAB LOBSTER CLASP

18" (45.7 CM) LENGTH OF 22-GAUGE (0.65 MM) TEAL NIOBIUM ROUND WIRE

FLUSH-CUT WIRE CUTTERS

FLAT-NOSED PLIERS

RIO JETSET ADHESIVE

1. Slip one of the end caps onto one end of the wire and secure with a dab of adhesive.

2. To the wire, add the following in this order: crimp bead, coin pearl, crimp bead, round pearl, crimp bead, square pearl, crimp bead, coin pearl, crimp bead.

3. Taking the flat-nosed pliers, **crimp** very tightly the first crimp bead 3/4" (1.9 cm) from the end of the wire with the end cap.

4. Slide the coin pearl next to this crimped bead and follow that with another crimp bead. Secure this crimp bead and **crimp** very tightly on the other side of the coin pearl. This will prevent the coin pearl from slipping down the wire of the necklace.

5. Slide the round pearl up the necklace and 1 1/2" (3.8 cm) from the second crimped bead. Add another crimp bead and **crimp** very tightly.

6. Slide the square pearl up the necklace and 1 1/2" (3.8 cm) from the third crimped bead. Add another crimp bead and **crimp** very tightly.

7. Slide the last coin pearl (for this side of the necklace) up the necklace and 2" (5.1 cm) from the fourth crimped bead. Add another crimp bead and **crimp** very tightly.

8. Now you are ready to add the cotter pins with the aluminum stops and round pearl spacers. Add the following: 3/4" (1.9 cm) light cotter pin, aluminum stop, 1" (2.5 cm) light cotter pin, aluminum stop, 1" (2.5 cm) heavy cotter pin, round pearl, 2" (5.1 cm) heavy cotter pin, round pearl, 1" (2.5 cm) heavy cotter pin, aluminum stop, 1" (2.5 cm) light cotter pin, aluminum stop, 3/4" (1.9 cm) light cotter pin, aluminum stop, 1" (2.5 cm) light cotter pin, aluminum stop, 1" (2.5 cm) heavy cotter pin, round pearl.

9. Add the central element, a 2" (5.1 cm) heavy cotter pin.

10. Repeat steps 2–8 in reverse order to create a symmetrical necklace.

11. Add the final end cap and secure with a dab of adhesive.

12. Add a jump ring to one end of the necklace and add the lobster clasp and a jump ring to the other end.

JEWELER'S TIP

A small round crimp bead securely flattened or crimped between flat-nosed pliers is one way to prevent a bead or stone from slipping down wire. Also, take care when working with niobium wire and pliers; the hard edges of the pliers can mar the wire's surface.

RED RUBBER LARIAT

Rubber comes in a variety of forms for the jewelry maker. Tubing, cording, and flat bands are three of the most popular. The colors are also quite varied and the price is quite reasonable. Rubber is a natural complement to hardware. In fact, it can even be found at the hardware store, just not in the variety you may need. The red rubber cord used for this necklace contrasts with blue heart trade beads. The metallic finish of aluminum and stainless steel adds an additional zing, making this lariat a bold statement.

MATERIALS

SIX 6 MM STAINLESS STEEL HEX NUTS

FORTY-FIVE 8 MM STAINLESS STEEL HEX NUTS

THIRTY-TWO 1/16" (1.6 MM) ALUMINUM STOPS

TWO ALUMINUM 3/4" (1.9 CM) TENSION SPRINGS

ONE ALUMINUM CROSS DOWEL JOINT CONNECTOR 3/4" x 3/8" (1.9 X 1 CM)

SEVENTEEN 8 MM BLUE HEART BEADS

33" (83.8 CM) LENGTH OF 2 MM RED RUBBER CORD

FLUSH-CUT WIRE CUTTERS

FLAT-NOSED PLIERS

1. Start by cutting the ends of the red rubber tubing on a bias to make stringing easier. You might need to grasp the end of the tubing with your flat-nosed pliers to ease it through the aluminum stops.

2. String the following groups of two patterns onto the red rubber tubing, alternating between the two patterns, and leaving approximately 1" (2.5 cm) of empty tubing between each group: A) aluminum stop, 8 mm hex nut, 8 mm hex nut, blue heart bead, 8 mm hex nut, aluminum stop; B) aluminum stop, 8 mm hex nut, blue heart bead, 8 mm hex nut, 8 mm hex nut, aluminum stop. String a total of thirteen groups in this section.

3. Thread both ends of the red rubber tubing through the center hole of the cross dowel joint connector.

4. To the one end of the tubing that ended with pattern B, add pattern A.

5. Thread this end through the aluminum tension spring.

6. To this same end of the tubing, add the following: 6 mm hex nut, aluminum stop, 6 mm hex nut, aluminum stop, 6 mm hex nut.

7. Creating a loop, pass this end back through the aluminum tension spring using your flat-nosed pliers to push it in securely.

8. To the other end of the tubing add pattern B.

9. Thread this end through the aluminum tension spring.

10. To this same end of the tubing, add the following: 6 mm hex nut, blue heart bead, 6 mm hex nut, blue heart bead, 6 mm hex nut.

11. Creating a loop, pass this end back through the aluminum tension spring using your flat-nosed pliers to push it in securely.

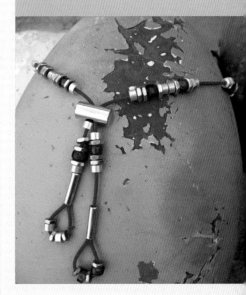

JEWELER'S TIP

I adjust the sections of hardware and beads so that the two loops are not hanging equally. The one end with the loop of blue hearts and hex nuts hangs slightly lower than the other. Of course, you can adjust the spacing a million different ways, creating a different look each time. The lariat can be short and worn close to the neck with longer ends or be fashioned to be a long loop with only short ends as shown here. The versatility of this necklace makes it all the more fun to wear.

This classic hardware store opened its doors in 1905 on Bridge Street in Great Barrington, Massachusetts. It was the typical turn-of-the-century hardware store, selling household goods as well as penny nails. It was known as Platt and Gossley's during the first half of the century until Harland Foster bought the store after World War II in 1947 and changed the name to Harland B. Foster, Inc. His two sons, Robert and Bill, took on the business in 1967. The eldest son, known familiarly as Bob, grew up around the store and assumed responsibility for the hardware. The sense of family and connection to the community is still visible today; regular customers fill out their own slips in a handwritten ledger book at the counter. The old wooden containers for fasteners hold a wide variety of hardware and the aisles of drawers provide hours of perusing enjoyment.

BRACELETS

CHAPTER

3

HEAVY HEX NUTS

A customer once called this bracelet "a party on a wrist," and I think it very appropriately describes the feeling it imparts when worn. The sparkle of the hex nut is accentuated by the iridescence of the Swarovski cube crystals. The natural luster of the pearls completes the design. Using stainless steel hex nuts will prevent any rust or corrosion. The stainless steel gives this bracelet a nice weight and prevents it from rusting or discoloring. Even though it is a substantial piece, it is still very comfortable to wear.

MATERIALS

FORTY-TWO 8 MM STAINLESS STEEL HEX NUTS

TWENTY-FIVE 6 MM STAINLESS STEEL HEX NUTS

SIXTEEN 5 MM PEACOCK NEARLY ROUND PEARLS

SIX 4 MM EMERALD GREEN SWAROVSKI CRYSTALS

TWO 4 MM LIGHT GREEN SWAROVSKI CRYSTALS

ONE 4 MM SAPPHIRE BLUE SWAROVSKI CRYSTALS

THREE 8 MM MONTANA SAPPHIRE SWAROVSKI CRYSTALS

TWO 8 MM SAPPHIRE BLUE SWAROVSKI CRYSTALS

7.5" (19.1 CM) LENGTH OF STERLING SILVER 2 MM ROLLO CHAIN

TWO 5 MM STERLING SILVER SPLIT RINGS

FOURTEEN 24-GAUGE (0.5 MM) 1 1/2" (3.8 CM) STERLING SILVER EYE PINS

SIXTEEN 24-GAUGE (0.5 MM) 1" (2.5 CM) STERLING SILVER HEAD PINS

ONE 12 MM STERLING SILVER LOBSTER CLASP

FLUSH-CUT WIRE CUTTERS

ROUND-NOSED PLIERS

FLAT-NOSED PLIERS

SPLIT RING PLIERS

1. Start by attaching one split ring to one of the ends of the sterling silver rollo chain.

2. Thread all of the 8 mm stainless steel hex nuts onto the rollo chain.

3. Attach the other split ring and the lobster clasp to the other end of the rollo chain. Attaching both split rings allows for an easier process of attaching the pearls and crystals without the hex nuts coming off of the chain.

4. Slip the sixteen peacock nearly round pearls onto sixteen separate 1" (2.5 cm) eye pins. Start a **wrap loop** for each, waiting to attach before the wraps are completed.

5. Slip the five 8 mm large cube crystals onto five separate 1 1/2" (3.8 cm) eye pins, adding one 6 mm hex nut to each eye pin. Start a **wrap loop** for each, waiting to attach before the wraps are completed.

6. Slip the nine 4 mm small cube crystals onto nine separate 1 1/2" (3.8 cm) eye pins, adding two 6 mm hex nuts to each eye pin. Start a **wrap loop** for each, waiting to attach before the wraps are completed.

7. You are now ready to add the wrap loops, which will be referred to as embellishments.

8. Starting from the lobster clasp end, attach the first peacock pearl to the second loop of the rollo chain.

9. Slide one of the hex nuts down to rest against this attached pearl and, counting up three loops, attach the next embellishment, one of the 4 mm dark green crystals with hex nuts.

10. Continue in this manner, sliding one or two hex nuts down the bracelet in an alternating pattern and attaching the next embellishment to the third loop up on the rollo chain.

11. I have alternated the peacock pearl embellishments with the crystal cube and hex nut embellishments in a consistent manner. Within this pattern, you can attach the crystal and hex nut embellishments in any order. The following is the order I used:

- two 4 mm emerald green crystals
- one 8 mm Montana sapphire crystal
- one 4 mm emerald green crystal
- one 8 mm sapphire blue crystal
- one 8 mm Montana sapphire crystal
- one 4 mm emerald green crystal
- one 4 mm light green crystal
- one 8 mm sapphire blue crystal
- one 4 mm emerald green crystal
- one 8 mm Montana sapphire crystal
- one 4 mm light green crystal
- one 4 mm emerald green crystal
- one 4 mm sapphire blue crystal

12. You should end with one of the peacock pearls. Complete the **wrap loops** and trim off the excess wire.

13. Attach the remaining peacock pearl to the split ring on the end of the chain opposite the lobster clasp and complete the **wrap loop**.

VARIATION

There are an infinite number of variations on this bracelet. Glass beads, assorted pearls and random leftovers can all be added as embellishments to create unique creations. This variation uses red coral branches and coin pearls. I call this "The Wilma" as the red coral reminds me of the *Flintstones* cartoon from my childhood.

JEWELER'S TIP

Using a random assortment of colors and sizes for the embellishments that are attached to the rollo chain creates a more dynamic bracelet. Whenever people look at this bracelet, they are always surprised when they discover a color that is not within a pattern that they assumed had existed. They finger the crystals, noticing the colors more; the random assortment makes each one more special.

VARIATION

This variation uses the same number of aluminum ferrules, but adds locking nuts to the design palette. The result is a more industrial and heavier-looking bracelet. The yellow and blue glass beads contrast with each other and add life to the matte finish of the hardware.

ALUMINUM AND GLASS

Aluminum hardware makes this bracelet one of my most lightweight hardware designs. The addition of recycled glass adds some weight, but the glass is very light in its effect. A Dremel is necessary to enlarge the holes of the glass in order to slide it onto the sterling chain. Blue and green recycled glass reminds me of beach glass found along the shore in summer.

MATERIALS

NINE 8 MM ALUMINUM FERRULES

SEVENTEEN 4 x 6 MM ALUMINUM STOPS

FOUR 8 MM GREEN RECYCLED GLASS BEADS

FOUR 8 MM BLUE RECYCLED GLASS BEADS

TEN 4 MM GREEN GLASS BEADS

TEN 4 MM BLUE GLASS BEADS

7" (17.8 CM) LENGTH OF STERLING SILVER 1.9 MM DRAWN FLAT CABLE CHAIN

3" (7.6 CM) LENGTH OF STERLING SILVER 2.5 MM ROUND CABLE CHAIN

TWO STERLING 5 MM STERLING SILVER SPLIT RINGS

SEVENTEEN 24-GAUGE (0.5 MM) 1 1/2" (3.8 CM) STERLING SILVER EYE PINS

ONE 24-GAUGE (0.5 MM) 2" (5.1 CM) STERLING SILVER EYE PIN

ONE 12-MM STERLING SILVER LOBSTER CLASP

DREMEL OR FLEX-SHAFT

FLUSH-CUT WIRE CUTTERS

ROUND-NOSED PLIERS

FLAT-NOSED PLIERS

SPLIT RING PLIERS

1. Start by **reaming** and enlarging the holes of the glass beads with a Dremel or flex-shaft. The holes will need to be approximately 3 mm wide. Set aside.

2. Attach one split ring to one of the ends of the sterling silver cable chain.

3. Thread eight of the 8 mm aluminum ferrules onto the cable chain, alternating with all of the 8 mm green and blue recycled glass beads.

4. Attach the other split ring and the lobster clasp to the other end of the rollo chain.

5. Slip seventeen aluminum stops onto seventeen separate 1" (2.5 cm) eye pins.

6. Onto nine of the aluminum stops add a blue 4 mm glass bead. Start a **wrap loop** for each, waiting to attach before the wraps are completed.

7. Onto eight of the aluminum stops add a green 4 mm glass bead. Start a **wrap loop** for each, waiting to attach before the wraps are completed.

8. Onto the 2" (5.1 cm) sterling silver eye pin, add a 4 mm blue glass bead, followed by an 8 mm aluminum ferrule and two 4 mm green glass beads. Start a **wrap loop**, waiting to attach before the wrap is completed.

9. Starting from the lobster clasp end, attach the aluminum stop dangle with a blue glass bead to the first loop of the cable chain.

10. Slide one of the aluminum ferrules down to rest against this attached dangle and attach the next dangle, alternating with a green glass one, onto the first fully exposed loop of the cable chain.

11. Continue in this manner, sliding one aluminum ferrule down the bracelet and attaching the next alternating color of dangle to the first fully exposed loop on the cable chain.

12. Complete all of the **wrap loops**, trimming off any excess wire.

13. Attach the remaining dangle, the one with the larger aluminum ferrule and three 4 mm glass beads to one end of the 3" (7.6 cm) section of round cable chain. Complete the **wrap loop**.

14. Attach the other end of the round cable chain to the split ring on the end of the chain opposite the lobster clasp.

JEWELER'S TIP

ATTACHING AN ADDITIONAL LENGTH TOF CHAIN TO ONE END OF THE BRACELET ALLOWS FOR ADJUST-ABILITY IN LENGTH. THIS IS THE REAL BENEFIT OF USING A LOBSTER CLAP INSTEAD OF A TOGGLE CLASP FOR A BRACELET. MAKE SURE WHEN YOU SELECT THAHT CHAIN THAT THE LOBSTER CLASP IS NOT TOO BIG FOR THE LOOPS OF THE CHAIN.

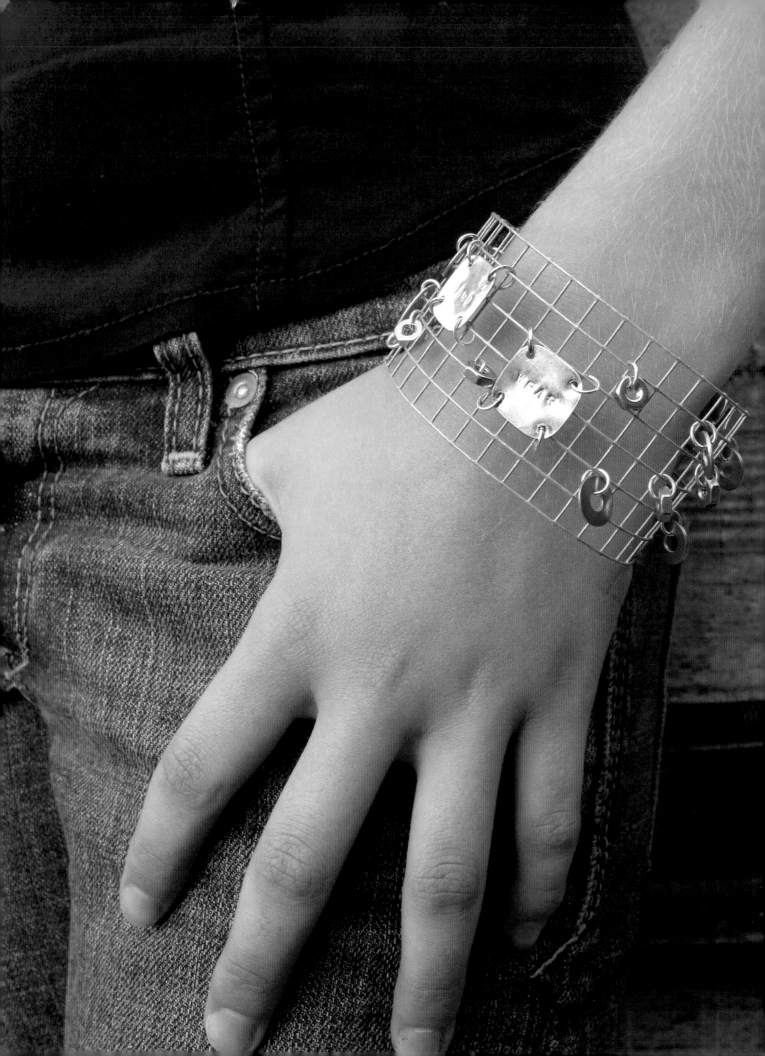

METAL GRID CUFF

MATERIALS

TEN 6 MM STAINLESS STEEL HEX NUTS

EIGHT 9 MM STAINLESS STEEL FLAT WASHERS

TWO 10 MM BRASS HEX NUTS

TWO 1/2" (1.3 CM) ALUMINUM SCREW POSTS (RIVETS)

8" (20.3 CM) LENGTH OF GALVANIZED STEEL CHICKEN WIRE GRID 1 1/2" (3.8 CM) WIDE

THREE 15 X 15 MM 26-GAUGE (3.5 MM) STERLING SILVER ROUNDED SQUARE STAMPING

FORTY-TWO 4 MM STERLING SILVER JUMP RINGS

HEAVY-DUTY WIRE CUTTERS

DRILL PRESS

1/16" (1.6 MM) DRILL BIT

SET OF LETTER STAMPS

BALL-PEEN HAMMER

BRACELET MANDREL

JEWELRY FILE

FLAT-NOSED PLIERS

Chicken wire is a great material for cuff bracelets as it is easy to form, but stiff enough to retain shape. The grid is perfect for all types of attachments and it is hardcore hardware at its best. The number of sterling silver square stampings will be determined by the message or names that are desired for each cuff bracelet. Likewise, the attached hardware will vary depending on the final design.

1. Start by cutting an 8" (20.3 cm) length of steel chicken wire, 1 1/2" (3.8 cm) wide. Cut as close to the edge as possible so that there will be less to file.

2. With the jewelry file, **file** smooth all of the rough ends of the chicken wire protruding from the four sides.

3. Using a bracelet mandrel, **bend** and shape the chicken wire to form a continuous circle.

4. Overlap the chicken wire ends by one grid section and pass the two grommets through the first and last grids, screwing on the nuts tightly to hold the bracelet in a closed circle.

5. Using a center punch, mark four holes in each corner of all three sterling silver square stampings.

6. With the 1/6" (1.6 mm) drill bit attached to the drill press, **drill** four holes for each of the three square stampings.

7. **File** the rough edges of the holes smooth, being careful not to mar the surface of the silver.

8. Carefully lining up the letters for each stamp, **stamp** the sterling silver squares with a ball-peen hammer and the letter stamping set.

9. With four jump rings, attach each sterling silver square to the chicken wire, attaching each jump ring at a cross section of wire.

10. Add the hex nuts and flat washers to thirty separate jump rings, attaching to the grid of chicken wire at random intervals.

JEWELER'S TIP

A DRILL PRESS IS AN IMPORTANT TOOL TO GET COMFORTABLE WITH BEFORE YOU START TO WORK ON EXPENSIVE MATERIALS OR IMPORTANT PIECES. IT IS REALLY QUITE EASY TO USE, BUT A FEW RULES MUST BE FOLLOWED. FIRST, WEAR SAFETY GOGGLES; THE SPURS FROM THE METAL CAN EASILY FLY UPWARD OFF OF THE DRILL PRESS. SECOND, USE A CLAMP, IF POSSIBLE. THE METAL CAN BECOME QUITE HEATED WHEN THE DRILL IS WORKING THE METAL. THIRD, ALWAYS USE A CENTER PUNCH TO GENTLY MARK THE LOCATION OF THE HOLES TO BE DRILLED; DO NOT HAMMER TOO STRONGLY AS IT CAN WARP THE METAL. AND FOURTH, DO NOT FORCE THE DRILL THROUGH THE METAL. IF YOU ARE USING A SHARP DRILL BIT WITH THE CORRECT SPEED, THE DRILL SHOULD DO THE WORK, NOT YOUR MUSCLES.

AS AN ALTERNATIVE, YOU CAN USE A DREMEL OR FLEX-SHAFT FOR THE DRILLING REQUIRED FOR THIS PROJECT. THE TECHNIQUE IS THE SAME. AFTER MARKING THE LOCATION TO BE DRILLED WITH A CENTER PUNCH, SECURE THE METAL TO BE DRILLED ON YOUR WORKBENCH AND DRILL THE HOLE WITH THE DREMEL OR FLEX-SHAFT.

LAYERS OF TUBES

Rubber tubing and memory wire can be combined in a variety of different ways for necklaces, bracelets, earrings, and other accessories. This bracelet was a design that kept evolving, adding more elements until it finally became a miniature solar system. I like wearing it wrapped all the way up my forearm; that way the individual "planets" can best be identified.

SIXTY-SIX 8 MM STAINLESS STEEL HEX NUTS

TWO 6 MM STAINLESS STEEL HEX NUTS

TWENTY-FOUR 9 MM STAINLESS STEEL FLAT WASHERS

FORTY-EIGHT 8 MM STAINLESS STEEL FLAT WASHERS

ONE 6 MM PICASSO JASPER BEAD

ONE 8 MM WHITE ROUND FRESHWATER PEARL

ONE 8 MM LAPIS LAZULI BEAD

ONE 10 MM GOLD FOIL BEAD

ONE 12 MM MALACHITE BEAD

ONE 12 MM BROWN OPAL BEAD

ONE 20 MM SPONGE CORAL BEAD

TWO 24-GAUGE (0.5 MM) 1 1/2" (3.8 CM) STERLING SILVER EYE PINS

44" (111.8 CM) LENGTH OF 24-GAUGE (0.5 MM) 2 1/8" (5.4 CM) DIAMETER STAINLESS STEEL MEMORY WIRE

40" (101.6 CM) LENGTH OF 2.5 MM (1.8 MM INSIDE DIAMETER) BLACK RUBBER TUBING

FLUSH-CUT WIRE CUTTERS

ROUND-NOSED PLIERS

FLAT-NOSED PLIERS

1. Cut the rubber tubing into sections so that you have two 5" (12.7 cm), two 7" (17.8 cm), and two 8" (20.3 cm) sections. Set aside.

2. Taking the eye pin, slip on the white round pearl followed by one of the 6 mm hex nuts. Start but do not complete a wrap loop. Set aside.

3. Taking the other eye pin, slip on the Picasso jasper bead followed by one of the 6 mm hex nuts. Start but do not complete a wrap loop. Set aside.

4. Using your round-nosed pliers, make a loop on one end of the memory wire so that once you start adding the rubber sections and the hardware, the wire doesn't slip into the tubing.

5. Guide the first section of rubber tubing, a 5" (12.7 cm) section, onto the memory wire and slide all the way to the end of the wire with the loop.

6. Add the hardware in the following order:

- hex nut
- 8 mm washer
- 9 mm washer
- 8 mm washer
- three hex nuts
- 8 mm washer
- 9 mm washer
- 8 mm washer
- three hex nuts
- 8 mm washer
- 9 mm washer
- 8 mm washer
- three hex nuts
- 8 mm washer
- 9 mm washer
- 8 mm washer
- hex nut

Slip these onto the rubber tubing at the end of the memory wire.

7. Add the malachite bead, sliding against the first section of tubing.

8. Guide the second section of rubber tubing, an 8" (20.3 cm) section, onto the memory wire and slide all the way to the malachite bead.

9. Repeat step 6.

10. Add the lapis lazuli bead, sliding against the second section of tubing.

11. Guide the third section of rubber tubing, a 7" (17.8 cm) section, onto the memory wire and slide all the way to the lapis lazuli bead.

12. Repeat step 6.

(continued on page 64)

13. Add the sponge coral bead, sliding against the third section of tubing.

14. Guide the fourth section of rubber tubing, an 8" (20.3 cm) section, onto the memory wire and slide all the way to the sponge coral bead.

15. Repeat step 6.

16. Add the gold foil bead, sliding against the fourth section of tubing.

17. Guide the fifth section of rubber tubing, a 7" (17.8 cm) section, onto the memory wire and slide all the way to the gold foil bead.

18. Repeat step 6.

19. Add the opal bead, sliding against the fifth section of tubing.

20. Guide the final section of rubber tubing, a 5" (12.7 cm) section, onto the memory wire and slide all the way to the opal bead.

21. Repeat step 6.

22. Make the final loop at the end of the memory wire to prevent the rubber tubing from slipping.

23. Onto one end of the memory wire, add one of the dangles you had set aside to end the loop of the bracelet, completing the wrap loop and trimming off any excess wire.

24. Repeat step 23 on the other end of the bracelet for the other dangle.

JEWELER'S TIP

END CAPS CAN BE USED FOR MEMORY WIRE TO COMPLETE THE BRACELET. YOU MUST BE SURE THAT THE END CAPS FIT SNUGGLY; I AFFIX THEM WITH AN EXTRA DAB OF ADHESIVE. SINCE THE RUBBER TUBING IS CUT INTO SECTIONS, IF THE END CAPS BECOME DETACHED FROM THE MEMORY WIRE, BUT REMAIN ATTACHED TO THE END OF THE TUBING, THE SECTIONS WILL SLIP AND WIRE CAN BE EXPOSED. I SOLVED THIS BY CREATING MY OWN LOOPS ON THE ENDS OF THE MEMORY WIRE, BUT KEEP IN MIND THAT THE WIRE IS HARD AND A STRONG HAND IS NEEDED TO FORM A LOOP.

BRAIDED LEATHER

Braided leather is a very sexy material. The roughness of the weave contrasted with the soft feel of natural leather is an appealing combination. Large brass hex nuts and washers have been threaded onto this bracelet and finished with a creative clasp. This design is sized for a man's wrist, but can easily be adapted to fit a woman's smaller size. The overall length is 9" (22.9 cm).

MATERIALS

THREE 9 MM BRASS HEX NUTS

NINE 11 MM BRASS HEX NUTS

TEN 14 MM BRASS FLAT WASHERS

TWO 3/4" (1.9 CM) BRASS INSERTS

TWO 3/16" (4.8 MM) RUBBER GROMMETS

ONE FEMALE FLARE ADAPTER 1/4" (6 MM) OUTSIDE DIAMETER X 1/4" (6 MM) FLARE

8" (20.3 CM) LENGTH OF FOUR-PLY BRAIDED BROWN LEATHER CORD

FLUSH-CUT WIRE CUTTERS

ROUND-NOSED PLIERS

FLAT-NOSED PLIERS

RIO JETSET ADHESIVE

1. Slide the two rubber grommets over the two brass inserts, pushing the grommets to the end of the insert, resting against the flared end.

2. Slide each insert into the two female receptacles of the female flare adapter. One of the grommets will be exposed within the female receptacle, but both should be snug inside the receptacle. Set aside.

3. Thread one 9 mm brass hex nut onto the braided leather, leaving 1" (2.5 cm) from one of the ends.

4. Thread onto the braided leather the following pattern: one 11 mm brass hex nut, three 14 mm brass flat washers, one 11 mm brass hex nut.

5. Add another 9 mm brass hex nut, leaving 2" (5.1 cm) of braided leather from the other 9 mm brass hex nut.

6. Thread onto the braided leather the following pattern:
   - one 11 mm brass hex nut
   - one 14 mm brass flat washer
   - one 11 mm brass hex nut
   - one 14 mm brass flat washer
   - one 11 mm brass hex nut
   - one 14 mm brass flat washer
   - one 11 mm brass hex nut
   - one 14 mm brass flat washer
   - one 11 mm brass hex nut

7. Add another 9 mm brass hex nut, leaving 3" (7.6 cm) of braided leather from the other 9 mm brass hex nut.

8. Thread onto the braided leather the following pattern: one 11 mm brass hex nut, three 14 mm brass flat washers, one 11 mm brass hex nut.

9. Add another 9 mm brass hex nut, leaving 2" (5.1 cm) of braided leather from the other 9 mm brass hex nut and 1" (2.5 cm) length from the end.

10. Insert both ends of the braided leather into the brass inserts and secure well with adhesive.

11. The bracelet will clasp by screwing the male connector into the female receptacle.

JEWELER'S TIP

USING SLIGHTLY SMALLER-DIAMETER HEX NUTS ALLOWS FOR THE MOVEMENT OF HARDWARE ONLY BETWEEN SECTIONS OF HEX NUTS. THE DIAMETER OF THE 9 MM HEX NUT IS SNUG ON THE BRAIDED LEATHER, PREVENTING ALL OF THE HARDWARE FROM TRAVELING TO ONE END OF THE BRACELET.

HARDWARE BLUES

This expansion bracelet is really fun to make and the base for the design is already constructed for you. A combination of stainless steel hex nuts and stainless steel lock nuts are the only hardware used, but the overall look is very mechanical because of the background of the expansion bracelet. Varieties of 3-mm blue glass beads naturally complement each other, but contrasting bright colors would also be a good choice.

MATERIALS

TEN 8-MM STAINLESS STEEL HEX NUTS

ELEVEN 8-MM STAINLESS STEEL LOCKING NUTS

ONE STAINLESS STEEL EXPANSION BRACELET 2" (5.1 CM) DIAMETER (AT REST)

TWENTY-ONE 3-MM ASSORTED BLUE GLASS BEADS

TWENTY-ONE 24-GAUGE (0.5 MM) 2" (5.1 CM) STERLING SILVER EYE PINS

FLUSH-CUT WIRE CUTTERS

ROUND-NOSED PLIERS

FLAT-NOSED PLIERS

1. Starting anywhere on the expansion bracelet, attach one of the end loops of eye pins to one of the links in the middle row of the bracelet. Close the loop tightly.

2. In the same manner, continue to attach all of the eye pins skipping every other link along the middle row of the bracelet. You will be left with a spiky row of eye pins sticking off the middle row of the bracelet.

3. Starting with any of the eye pins, slide one of the lock nuts onto the eye pin followed by a blue glass bead.

4. Start and complete a **wrap loop**, snuggly anchoring the blue glass bead and the nut to the link of the expansion bracelet.

5. Working down the line, alternate hex nut with locking nut followed by the assortment of glass beads. I have used four different hues of blue in this project.

6. The row will end with a locking nut next to the first locking nut that you attached, but they should have different blue glass beads.

JEWELER'S TIP

There is an alternate and more traditional way of attaching the eye pins to the links of the expansion bracelet. You can assemble all of your attachments on eye pins or head pins, starting but not completing the wrap loops. Then you can attach the wrap loop to the link of the expansion bracelet and complete the wrap. The attachments will dangle from the bracelet instead of being snuggly fitted to the bracelet. It is a very different look.

IN THE EARLY 1900s, CULPEPER, VIRGINIA, SUPPORTED THREE HARDWARE
STORES WITHIN A THREE-BLOCK RADIUS OF THE TRAIN STATION. CULPEPER WAS
AN IMPORTANT RAILROAD DEPOT FOR THE REGION, CONNECTING THE FARMS
OF THE VIRGINIA PIEDMONT TO THE MARKETS OF THE NORTH AND SOUTH.
TODAY, ONE HARDWARE STORE REMAINS, CLARKE HARDWARE, AND IT HAS
BEEN IN CONTINUOUS OPERATION WITH ONLY TWO OWNERS SINCE 1906. THE
FRONT OF THE STORE HAS A WELCOMING DISPLAY OF TRICYCLES, WAGONS, AND
VEGETABLES. AFTER YOU ENTER THROUGH THE NINE-FOOT DOOR INTO A SPACE
WITH FOURTEEN-FOOT TIN CEILINGS, YOU ARE GREETED BY THE CURRENT OWNER,
THE VERY FRIENDLY CLAUDE MINNICH. MR. MINNICH BOUGHT THE STORE FROM
MRS. CLARKE IN 1980 AND HAS BEEN TAKING CARE OF THE LOCAL HARDWARE
NEEDS EVER SINCE. AN UNUSUAL DISPLAY OF CORKS INTRIGUED ME; SMALL
DIAMETER NATURAL CORKS AND LARGE RUBBER CORKS REPRESENTS HARDWARE
IN PURE FORM WAITING FOR IMAGINATION.

EARRINGS

COIL SPRING DROPS

These easy earrings are very fun to wear. I use stainless steel springs in a wide assortment of widths and lengths. The loops on both ends make them a natural component of an earring. I always think of my screen door in Connecticut when I wear these, recalling good memories of long summer days.

MATERIALS

TWO 2 1/2" (6.4 CM) 1/8" (3 MM) EXPANSION SPRINGS

TEN 3 MM COPPER DISKS

TWO 12 MM WHITE COIN PEARLS

TWO 24-GAUGE (0.5 MM) 1 1/2" (3.8 CM) STERLING SILVER BALL-TIP PINS

TWO 21-GAUGE (0.7 MM) STERLING SILVER FRENCH EAR WIRES

FLUSH-CUT WIRE CUTTERS

ROUND-NOSED PLIERS

FLAT-NOSED PLIERS

1. Start by attaching the expansion spring to the French wire, closing both loops securely.

2. Slip one white coin pearl onto one 1 1/2" (3.8 cm) ball-tip pin.

3. To this ball-tip pin, add five copper disks.

4. Start a **wrap loop**, and attach to the free end of the expansion spring.

5. Complete the wrap, and cut off the excess wire.

6. Repeat to create a matching pair.

VARIATION

You can vary the dangles that are attached to the expansion springs in infinite ways. You can also vary the size spring. Remember your proportions are important; if you use a fatter spring, you might want to consider a more substantial dangle. This variation uses 1 1/2" (3.8 cm) 1/4" (6 mm) expansion springs, with center drilled coin pearls topped with green recycled glass, aluminum ferrules, and small blue beads.

JEWELER'S TIP

MAKE SURE THAT YOU CLOSE THE LOOP OF THE EXPANSION SPRING WHEN ATTACHING TO EITHER THE LOOP OF THE FRENCH WIRE EARRING OR THE LOOP OF THE DANGLE. OFTEN THE LOOP ON THE SPRING IS NOT COMPLETELY CLOSED AND WITHOUT CARE YOU COULD LOSE AN EARRING OR DANGLE.

ASSORTED NUTS

Nuts and bolts—well, at least nuts—form the basic structure for many of my designs. There are so many different combinations of sizes, types, materials; digging through them in hardware stores has occupied me for many hours. I love stacks of the tiny ones and the way the square nuts twist and turn. But my all-time favorites are the wing nuts; my son thinks these earrings look like missiles, and I guess that is a cool thing.

MATERIALS

TWO 10 MM STAINLESS
STEEL WING NUTS

TWO 8 MM STAINLESS
STEEL HEX NUTS

TWO 6 MM STAINLESS
STEEL HEX NUTS

TWO 10 MM SILVER FOIL
BEADS

TWO 8 MM BLUE FOIL
BEADS

TWO 6 MM BLUE GLASS
BEADS

TWO 24-GAUGE (0.5 MM)
2" (5.1 CM) STERLING
SILVER EYE PINS

TWO 21-GAUGE (0.7 MM)
STERLING SILVER FRENCH
EAR WIRES

FLUSH-CUT WIRE CUTTERS

ROUND-NOSED PLIERS

FLAT-NOSED PLIERS

1. Stack onto one of the eye pins the following: 8 mm blue foil bead, wing nut, 10 mm silver foil bead, 8 mm hex nut, 6 mm hex nut, 6 mm blue bead.

2. Start and complete a **wrap loop**.

3. Open the loop of the French ear wire and attach to the loop of the eye pin.

4. Repeat steps 1–3 to make a matching pair.

VARIATION

I have used stainless steel, bronze, brass, and gold-plated nuts in dimensions ranging from 4 mm to 10 mm. The variations combine the simple hardware of assorted nuts with Swarovski crystals, glass foil beads, freshwater pearls, lapis lazuli, carnelian, amethyst, and rose quartz. The possibilities are indeed limitless.

VARIATION

This variation is created from brass and copper hardware. Brass is a more malleable material, so be careful when you drill the holes as the metal is easily warped by the drill press.

WASHER DANGLE

Round flat washers coupled with spiky lock washers give these earrings a geometric look. The size of the washers will determine how bold the statement, but the strength of the design is not subtle. Vary the material to complement your attire. The earrings are connected with large jump rings in order to maintain a proper proportion and also to allow for the drilling of the holes not too close to the edge.

1. With a center punch, mark the locations of the holes to be drilled, using a steady solid motion with a ball-peen hammer.

2. Using a 1/16" (1.6 mm) drill bit, **drill** two holes on opposite sides of the 14-mm and 18 mm flat washers.

3. Using the same drill bit, **drill** one hole in the top of the large 3.1-cm flat washer.

4. **File** all rough edges of the drilled holes with a jewelry file.

5. Attach the large 3.1 cm flat washer to the 18 mm flat washer with an 8 mm jump ring, adding the 15 mm lock washer before closing the ring.

6. Attach the 18 mm flat washer to the 14 mm flat washer with an 8 mm jump ring, adding the 13 mm lock washer before closing the ring.

7. Attach another 8 mm jump ring to the 14 mm flat washer, adding the 8-mm lock washer before closing the ring.

8. Open the loop of the French ear wire and attach the earring by the 5 mm jump ring.

9. Repeat steps 1–8 to make a matching pair.

JEWELER'S TIP

Again, if you do not own a drill press or are not comfortable with its use, you can drill the holes in the washers using a Dremel or flex-shaft.

MATERIALS

- TWO 3.1 CM STAINLESS STEEL FLAT WASHERS
- TWO 18 MM STAINLESS STEEL FLAT WASHERS
- TWO 14 MM STAINLESS STEEL FLAT WASHERS
- TWO 15 MM STAINLESS STEEL LOCK WASHERS
- TWO 13 MM STAINLESS STEEL INTERIOR LOCK WASHERS
- TWO 8 MM STAINLESS STEEL LOCK WASHERS
- TWO 24 GAUGE (0.5 MM) 5 MM STERLING SILVER JUMP RINGS
- SIX 24-GAUGE (0.5 MM) 8 MM STERLING SILVER JUMP RINGS
- TWO 21-GAUGE (0.7 MM) STERLING SILVER FRENCH EAR WIRES
- DRILL PRESS
- 1/16" (1.6 MM) DRILL BIT
- JEWELRY FILE
- FLAT-NOSED PLIERS

ALUMINUM AND PEARLS

The sterling silver rollo chain adds length and flexibility to these dangle earrings. The luster of the freshwater pearls complements the matte sheen of the aluminum ferrules. Proportion is the key to the design.

MATERIALS

TWO 8 MM ALUMINUM FERRULES

FOUR 4 X 6 MM ALUMINUM STOPS

TWO 8 MM STAINLESS STEEL LOCK WASHERS

TWO 12 MM WHITE COIN PEARLS

TWO 24-GAUGE (0.5 MM) 2" (5.1 CM) STERLING SILVER HEAD PINS

TWO 21-GAUGE (0.7 MM) STERLING SILVER FRENCH EAR WIRES

2" (5.1 CM) LENGTH OF STERLING SILVER 2 MM ROLLO CHAIN

FLUSH-CUT WIRE CUTTERS

ROUND-NOSED PLIERS

FLAT-NOSED PLIERS

1. Cut the rollo chain into two equal sections and attach each section to the loops of the French ear wires.

2. Slide the coin pearl onto one of the head pins, followed by an aluminum stop, a washer, and another aluminum stop. Start a **wrap loop**.

3. Thread one of the aluminum ferrules onto the rollo chain with the wider opening facing down.

4. Attach the loop of the head pin to the free end of the rollo chain and complete the **wrap loop**. Trim off excess wire.

5. Repeat steps 2–4 to make a matching pair of earrings.

VARIATION

This variation uses hex nuts in addition to aluminum ferrules and substitutes peacock round pearls for the white coin pearls. The section of chain is also half as long as the other project. I like the alternation of the hardware and the proportions of the elements.

JEWELER'S TIP

ALUMINUM FERRULES AND STOPS HAVE ONE OPENING THAT IS LARGER AND BEVELED. IT IS ALWAYS IMPORTANT TO RECOGNIZE THE DISTINCTION AND BE CONSISTENT IN THE DIRECTION USED. THE LARGER, BEVELED OPENING RESTS AGAINST THE LOOP OF THE ATTACHED DANGLE. IT SITS BETTER WITH THE BEVELED CIRCLE. SOMETIMES THE SMALLER OPENING IS REQUIRED, AS THE LARGER OPENING CAN SWALLOW UP A SMALL BEAD OR GEMSTONE.

VARIATION

This variation uses a slightly smaller light bulb and brass washers and wire. The bulb is also facing upwards, instead of down. The brass wire is always work-hardened as it is much more malleable than sterling silver.

80

BULB DANGLE

MATERIALS

TWO ROUND-HEAD FLASH-LIGHT BULBS

TWO 22 MM STAINLESS STEEL FLAT WASHERS (INSIDE DIAMETER OF 9 MM)

TWO 13 MM RUBBER GASKETS (INSIDE DIAMETER OF 6 MM)

8" (20.3 CM) LENGTH OF 21-GAUGE (0.7 MM) STERLING SILVER WIRE

DRILL PRESS

1/16" (1.6 MM) DRILL BIT

BALL-PEEN HAMMER

JEWELRY FILE

RING MANDREL

ROUND-NOSED PLIERS

FLAT-NOSED PLIERS

No they do not light up, but they are quite the conversation piece. These earrings incorporate a variety of techniques, but are really quite easy to make. Once you have mastered the drill press and the bending and forming of wire, all that is left is assembling the pieces. Figure out how to attach an LED light and you will definitely be the hit of the party.

1. Using a 1/16" (1.6 mm) drill bit, **drill** two holes in the opposite sides of the 22 mm flat washers.

2. **File** all rough edges of the drilled holes with a jewelry file.

3. Slide the washer over the threaded end of the light bulb, and then stretch the rubber gasket on, pushing it securely against the washer and bulb. Repeat for the other bulb and set aside.

4. Cut the sterling silver wire in half and **file** one end of each wire to a point, smoothing out any roughness.

5. With the round-nosed pliers, make a **simple loop** on the other end of each wire section.

6. Using the ring mandrel, bend both sections of the wire in a gentle circle, leaving a length of 1/4" (6 mm) extending below the ends with the loop. Both sections should be identical.

7. Using the round-nosed pliers, **bend** the extended lengths in a slight curve in the opposite direction of the circle.

8. Lay the pieces on a firm work surface, and hammer both sections of sterling silver wire to work-harden the metal.

9. Slide one section of the sterling silver wire through one of the holes of the washer. The end with the loop should rest under one of the holes of the washer, supporting the washer with the bulb end facing downward. The other end of wire, the section with the extended "tail," will complete the circle and tuck into the other drilled hole of the washer to close.

10. Repeat the final step to make a matching pair.

JEWELER'S TIP

Sterling silver wire is sold in a variety of diameters and types. "Half-hard" is a type used for the formation of jump rings, earring wires, and clasps. It is malleable enough to form, but generally strong enough to maintain its shape. "Work-hardening" metal is the process by which metal is worked, such as by striking with a hammer, which realigns the molecules and makes the metal more brittle. The result of work-hardening is a less malleable metal that is more resistant to bending.

HOOP OF HARDWARE

Hoop earrings are always in style. These large hoops have a simple palette of color and material. The use of all 8 mm hardware maintains an even rhythm in the design which is punctuated by simple peacock freshwater pearl dangles.

MATERIALS

SEVEN 8 MM STAINLESS STEEL HEX NUTS

FOURTEEN 8 MM STAINLESS STEEL FLAT WASHERS

FOURTEEN 8 MM STAINLESS STEEL LOCK WASHERS

EIGHT 6 MM PEACOCK FRESHWATER PEARLS

FOUR 4 MM PEACOCK FRESHWATER PEARLS

TWELVE 24-GAUGE (0.5 MM) 1" (2.5 CM) STERLING SILVER EYE PINS

TWO LARGE STERLING SILVER HOOP EARRINGS

FLUSH-CUT WIRE CUTTERS

ROUND-NOSED PLIERS

FLAT-NOSED PLIERS

1. Slide the twelve freshwater pearls onto twelve separate 1" (2.5 cm) sterling silver head pins. Start and complete a **wrap loop** for each. Set aside.

2. Add the following hardware to one of the hoop earrings: lock washer, flat washer, hex nut, flat washer, lock washer, 4 mm pearl dangle, lock washer, flat washer.

3. Add the following pattern: hex nut, flat washer, lock washer, 6 mm pearl dangle, lock washer, flat washer.

4. Repeat the step 3 pattern in three more times.

5. Complete the symmetry by adding: hex nut, flat washer, lock washer, pearl dangle, lock washer, flat washer, hex nut, flat washer, lock washer.

6. Repeat steps 2–5 to make a matching pair.

VARIATION

JEWELER'S TIP

Over long periods of time, these earrings are quite heavy to wear. Lessening the number of hex nuts in the pattern will lighten them considerably, but will change the proportion of the overall design.

Smaller hoops and lighter gauge hardware make these variations an easy alternative. The aluminum stops and flat washers offset the center drilled coin pearls, creating a relaxed, but elegant design.

CHAIN DANGLES

These are absolutely my favorite earrings for using leftover bits of hardware. Most small fasteners can be slipped onto head pins or adapted to hang from jump rings. The pearls and trade beads add color and light accentuating the natural shimmer of the metal. I love the way they jangle in the breeze sounding almost like wind chimes.

1. Cut the rollo chain into the following sections: four 1" (2.5 cm) sections, two 2" (5.1 cm) sections, two 1 1/2" (3.8 cm) sections, and two 1/2" (1.3 cm) sections.

2. Slide a round pearl followed by a 6 mm square nut, an 8 mm lock washer, a 6 mm hex nut, and a blue trade bead onto a head pin and start a **wrap loop**.

3. Slide a coin pearl followed by an 8 mm lock washer, a 6 mm hex nut, and a red trade bead onto a head pin and start a **wrap loop**.

4. Slide a round pearl followed by a 4 mm hex nut and a bronze ring onto a head pin and start a **wrap loop**.

5. Repeat steps 2–4 so that there are two sets of dangles and set aside.

6. Onto one jump ring, slide sections of chain in the following order: 1/2" (1.3 cm), 2" (5.1 cm), 1" (2.5 cm), 1 1/2" (3.8 cm), 1" (2.5 cm). Close the jump ring completely with the flat-nosed pliers.

7. Attach the jump ring with the chain dangles to a French ear wire and close the loop securely.

8. To the 1/2" (1.3 cm) section of chain, add a jump ring containing two 6 mm hex nuts and one 11 mm flat washer.

9. To the 2" (5.1 cm) section of chain, add the dangle with the round pearl and blue bead. Complete the **wrap loop**.

10. To the next section of chain, one of the 1" (2.5 cm) sections, add a jump ring containing one 16 mm lock washer, two 8 mm lock washers, and two 3 mm bronze rings.

11. To the 1 1/2" (3.8 cm) section of chain, add the dangle containing the coin pearl and the red bead. Complete the **wrap loop**.

12. To the last section of chain, one of the 1" (2.5 cm) sections, add the dangle with the round pearl and small hex nut and bronze ring. Complete the **wrap loop**.

13. Repeat steps 6–12 to make a matching pair.

MATERIALS

EIGHT 6 MM STAINLESS STEEL HEX NUTS

TWO 4 MM STAINLESS STEEL HEX NUTS

TWO 6 MM SQUARE NUTS

TWO 11 MM STAINLESS STEEL FLAT WASHERS

EIGHT 8 MM STAINLESS STEEL LOCK WASHERS

TWO 16 MM STAINLESS STEEL LOCK WASHERS

SIX 3 MM BRONZE RINGS

TWO 12 MM WHITE COIN PEARLS

FOUR 8 MM ROUND PEARLS

TWO 3 MM RED TRADE BEADS

TWO 3 MM BLUE TRADE BEADS

SIX 24-GAUGE (0.5 MM) 1" (2.5 CM) STERLING SILVER HEAD PINS

SIX 21-GAUGE (0.7 MM) 8 MM STERLING SILVER JUMP RINGS

TWO 21-GAUGE (0.7 MM) STERLING SILVER FRENCH EAR WIRES

12" (30.5 CM) LENGTH OF STERLING SILVER 2 MM ROLLO CHAIN

FLUSH-CUT WIRE CUTTERS

ROUND-NOSED PLIERS

FLAT-NOSED PLIERS

VARIATION

The variations on this theme are only limited by what is in your toolbox. You can attach any leftover bits of hardware and the earrings do not even have to be symmetrical. This variation uses brass chain and brass and copper fasteners combined with white freshwater pearls and carnelian.

The Nantucket Ship Chandlery is located on the wharf in Nantucket Harbor and supplies marine hardware to all the yachtsmen, fishermen, and small boaters on the island. Brass fittings of all types and sizes can be found here and many are easily adapted to create unique pieces of jewelry. The Chandlery was originally known as The Grey Lady of the Sea and has witnessed Nantucket's transformation from the sleepy outpost of a past whaling community to one of the most fashionable vacation destinations on the East Coast. In 1978, it was incorporated and became the Nantucket Ship Chandlery. Ellen Tonkin started working at the Chandlery shortly after the name change in 1980; she and her husband, Kim, bought the business eight years later. The Tonkins run a no-nonsense business, and while accommodating all the tourist traffic, know that their true customers are the fishermen and boat lovers that live on this island year-round.

ACCESSORIES

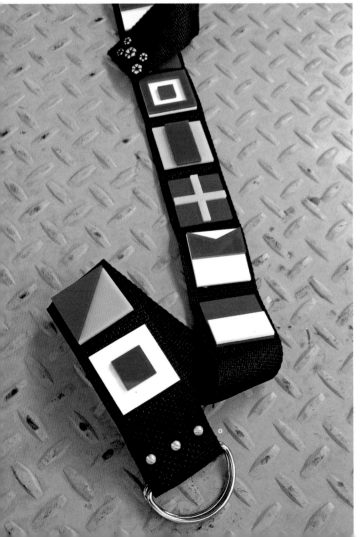

SIGNAL FLAG BELT

Signal flags have been used in nautical communication since the eighteenth century. They identify ships and vessels and can send messages by displaying an array of flags. Each flag or symbol represents a letter of the alphabet or shown individually, a condition on board the vessel. A red and white split field stands for the letter **H** or represents that the pilot is on board. A red diamond shape in a white field stands for the letter **F** or sends the alert that the boat is disabled. A yellow and red triangle stands for the letter **O** or signals that a man is overboard. This belt spells out **SOFTHARDWEAR**, the name of my line of hardware jewelry, but your belt can send any message you can assemble. Of course, always be careful what signals you send.

TWELVE 1 1/2" (3.8 CM) ACRYLIC NAUTICAL SIGNAL FLAG TILES

THREE 3/8" (1 CM) BRASS ROUND SLOTTED MACHINE SCREWS

FOUR 8 MM BRASS HEX NUTS

THREE 6 MM BRASS HEX NUTS

ONE 10 MM BRASS HEX NUT

TWO 2" (5.1 CM) BRASS D-RINGS

38" (96.5 CM) LENGTH OF 1 7/8" (4.7 CM) BLACK WEB BELTING

8' (243.8 CM) LENGTH OF BLACK NYLON THREAD

NEEDLE

LEATHER PUNCH

RIO JETSET ADHESIVE

1. Using the nylon thread and needle, whip-stitch the two ends of the web belting to prevent fraying.

2. Taking one end of the web belting, make a fold 2" (5.1 cm) from the end, tucking 3/4" (1.9 cm) back under the first fold so that the edge is not visible.

3. Slip on the pair of D-rings and hold the folds in one hand while you complete the next step.

4. Measuring 1" (2.5 cm) from this end use the **leather punch**, to punch a hole through the three layers of web belting in the center of the width of belting.

5. Insert a machine screw through this hole and secure with a hex nut on the back side of the belt.

6. Add two more holes, using the **leather punch**, punching to either side of the center hole. Insert screws, and secure with hex nuts.

7. Add a small dab of adhesive to each of the interior holes of the hex nuts once they are adjusted equally and securely.

8. Using the remaining thread and a needle, sew onto the other end five of the remaining assorted brass hex nuts.

9. Measuring 1" (2.5 cm) from the three machine screws and hex nuts, lay out the tiles of signal flags, allowing even spacing between them.

10. Peel off the back of each tile as you work your way from one end to the other, making sure that you have the tile facing the correct direction.

11. Once the tiles are adhered to the web belting, gently raise each corner of the tile and add a small dab of the adhesive. This will secure the tile completely.

(See page 87 for a full view of the belt)

JEWELER'S TIP

THERE ARE MANY WAYS OF EMBELLISHING THE END OF THE SIGNAL FLAG BELT AND A DECISION NEEDS TO BE MADE WHETHER TO SEW HEX NUTS ON THE FRONT OR BACK OF THE BELT. AS YOU FEED THE BELT BACK THROUGH THE D-RING, THE TOP OF THE BELT WILL BECOME THE UNDERSIDE. I EMBELLISH THE FRONT OF THE BELT, BECAUSE WHEN I PASS THE BELT THROUGH THE D-RING, I ALSO FOLD IT DOWN, CREATING A RIGHT-ANGLE TRIANGLE, AND TUCK THE EDGE UNDER THE D-RING. THIS KEEPS IT FROM SLIPPING AND ADDS A BIT MORE INTEREST TO THE BELT. IF YOU ARE NOT SURE HOW YOU WILL WEAR THE BELT, A SIMPLE SOLUTION IS JUST TO EMBELLISH BOTH SIDES, LINING UP THE HEX NUTS BACK TO BACK.

BLACK CHAIN BELT

The black-coated metal chain is trendy and elegant at the same time. The aluminum screw posts are used most frequently in scrapbooking and, coupled with the split rings, they add metallic elements to the design. A large lapis lazuli stone I found in Europe makes the belt unique. The final length of this belt will be 30" (76.2 cm) long, but with additional split rings, the belt can be adjusted to any length. Simply add more split rings and hex nuts accordingly.

MATERIALS

4' 10" (147.3 CM) LENGTH OF 3/4" (1.9 CM) BLACK-COATED METAL CHAIN

TEN 8 MM STAINLESS STEEL HEX NUTS

SIX 1/2" (1.3 CM) ALUMINUM SCREW POSTS (RIVETS)

FOUR 7/8" (2.2 CM) DIAMETER SPLIT RINGS

ONE 1 1/4" x 3/4" (3.1 x 1.9 CM) STAINLESS STEEL TWIST TOGGLE

3" (7.6 MM) LENGTH OF STERLING SILVER WIRE

ONE 30 x 20 MM TOP-DRILLED LAPIS LAZULI STONE

HEAVY-GAUGE WIRE CUTTERS

SPLIT RING PLIERS

RIO JETSET ADHESIVE

1. Start by cutting the black-coated chain in half with the heavy-gauge wire cutters.

2. Using the split ring pliers, thread one end of each chain and the five hex nuts onto the split ring.

3. Lay the two sections of chain out so that the loops align next to each other.

4. Count three loops of the chains from the end, thread the first aluminum screw post into this loop, and secure with the other end of the post.

5. Being careful to keep the chains aligned, count five loops of the chains, and thread the second aluminum screw post into this loop, and secure with the other end of the post.

6. Continue to keep the chains aligned. Count eight loops of the chains, thread the third aluminum screw post into this loop, and secure with the other end of the post.

7. At the other end, you should have equal lengths of chain. If not, cut off any extra loops so that the chains are the same length.

8. Count five loops of the chains from the end, thread the fourth aluminum screw post into this loop, and secure with the other end of the post.

9. Count five loops of the chains, thread the fifth aluminum screw post into this loop, and secure with the other end of the post.

10. Count eight loops of the chains, thread the final aluminum screw post into this loop, and secure with the other end of the post.

11. Once the posts are completed, add a small drop of adhesive to the exterior of the post. This will prevent it from unscrewing.

12. Slip the twisted toggle through the ends of the chains opposite the split ring. The toggle can then be attached to the split ring by screwing in the dowel of the toggle.

13. Add three split rings (you may add more as required) to the split ring attached to the chain. Add five hex nuts to the second of these split rings (if adding more than three split rings, simply add five hex nuts to every other split ring).

14. Create a **wire bail wrap** for the lapis lazuli stone and attach to the final split ring.

VARIATION

This variation uses another type of chain from the hardware store, a brass-tone base metal chain. The heavy brass clip is from a marine hardware store and the rivets that join the chain are heavy 3/4" (1.9 cm) bolts with hex nuts. The final dangle element is a large 32 mm antique Chinese turquoise bead.

JEWELER'S TIP

Do not use your expensive jeweler's tools to cut heavy-gauge wire from the hardware store. This is one time when a trip to the basement is necessary. My jeweler's quality flush wire cutter is my most prized tool; I spent a lot of money on it and I keep it in excellent condition. If you use this tool for jobs for which it is not intended, it will dull and the tip will wear, making fine cuts impossible. Use the industrial grade tool when necessary and save yourself the pain of replacement.

FLUORESCENT RUBBER ANKLET

This colorful anklet is easily adapted to a bracelet or choker. The addition of a length of chain makes it easily adjustable. I have chosen an assortment of primary colored beads to contrast with the bright apple green rubber; the possibilities are only limited by your bead box.

MATERIALS

TEN 6 MM STAINLESS STEEL HEX NUTS

THREE 6 MM BRASS HEX NUTS

NINE LOCK WASHERS

TWO 4 X 8 MM BRASS SPRING COILS

TWENTY-SEVEN ASSORTED 4 MM BEADS

TWENTY-FIVE 24-GAUGE (0.5 MM) 1" (2.5 CM) STERLING SILVER HEAD PINS

ONE 24-GAUGE (0.5 MM) 2" (5.1 CM) STERLING SILVER EYE PIN

TWO 4 MM STERLING SILVER SPLIT RINGS

TWO 10 MM STERLING SILVER PINCH CLASPS

ONE 8 X 14 MM STERLING SILVER LOBSTER CLASP

2" (5.1 CM) LENGTH OF 5.2 MM STERLING SILVER HAMMERED CHAIN

7" (17.8 CM) LENGTH OF 2 X 10 MM FLUORESCENT GREEN FLAT RUBBER

FLUSH-CUT WIRE CUTTERS

ROUND-NOSED PLIERS

FLAT-NOSED PLIERS

SPLIT RING PLIERS

LEATHER PUNCH

RULER

1. Add the two pinch clasps to both ends of the flat rubber. Secure firmly with flat-nosed pliers.

2. Cut the two brass spring coils into thirds. Set aside.

3. Measure 1/8" (3 mm) from the end of the pinch clasp and mark off points with a pencil down the centerline of the rubber in increments of 1/4" (6 mm).

4. Using the **leather punch**, align the points and punch twenty-five holes down the length of the rubber.

5. Into the first hole, poke a 1" (2.5 cm) head pin, pulling completely so that the end is flush with the rubber.

6. Slip on a stainless steel hex nut followed by one of the 4 mm colorful beads.

7. Bend the head pin above the bead 45 degrees. Trim off excess wire so that you have only 1/8" (3 mm) remaining. Make a **simple loop** with this end of wire to firmly secure the hardware and bead to the rubber.

8. Repeat steps 5–7, alternating hardware and colored beads. I have used a lock washer (which may need a slightly larger bead to cover) every third hole and have alternated the stainless steel hex nuts with brass coils or hex nuts.

9. To one end of the anklet, add a split ring and the lobster clasp.

10. To the other end of the anklet, add a split ring and the length of chain.

11. Finally, onto the 2" (5.1 cm) eye pin add a bead followed by a stainless steel hex nut, a lock washer, a section of brass coil, and a different color bead. Start a **wrap loop** and attach this wrap to the end of the adjustable chain. Complete the wrap, trimming off the excess wire.

JEWELER'S TIP

OFTEN FLAT RUBBER OR RUBBER CORD ARRIVES BENT OR IN COILS. IT IS SIMPLE TO STRAIGHTEN; DIP IT IN BOILING WATER FOR TWO MINUTES FOLLOWED BY A COLD BATH FOR THE SAME AMOUNT OF TIME. THIS WILL PREVENT FRUSTRATION AS YOU ARE DESIGNING OR WORKING WITH THIS FUN MATERIAL.

MESH RING

Black anodized aluminum is a great material for a variety of projects. This project could easy be fabricated to become a bracelet or even a belt. The rubber tubing prevents the edges from fraying over time and also protects against rough edges abrading the skin. The uniform round and flat brass washers contrast with the grid of the black material.

MATERIALS

ELEVEN 8 MM BRASS FLAT WASHERS

ELEVEN 4 MM BRASS JUMP RINGS

4" (10.2 CM) LENGTH OF 1" (2.5 CM)-WIDE BLACK ALUMINUM SCREENING MATERIAL

1" (2.5 CM) LENGTH OF 2.5 MM (1.8 MM INSIDE DIAMETER) BLACK RUBBER TUBING

1 1/2" (3.8 CM) LENGTH OF 21-GAUGE (0.7 MM) BRASS WIRE

FLUSH-CUT WIRE CUTTERS

ROUND-NOSED PLIERS

FLAT-NOSED PLIERS

RING MANDREL

PRECISION SCISSORS

RULER

RIO JETSET ADHESIVE

1. Using the straight edge of a ruler, make two folds, 1/4" (6 mm) wide, down the length of the screening material. Fold toward the center of the screening material, pressing flat.

2. Trim off 1/2" (1.3 cm) from each end. The band of screen should now be 1/2" (1.3 cm) wide and 2 1/2" (6.4 cm) long.

3. Cut the rubber tubing in two sections of 1/2" (1.3 cm).

4. Using scissors cut a slit in each section down the entire length of the tubing.

5. Insert each end of the screening material into the separate slits and affix with adhesive along each edge.

6. Add the flat washers to eleven separate jump rings, attaching to the mesh of screening material at random intervals.

7. Holding the round-nosed pliers with the jaws closed together, wrap the brass wire around both rounded jaws, creating 10 mm oval loops. Cut the loops into three jump rings.

8. Weave the oval jump rings through the mesh, wrapping around both bands of rubber tubing and closing in the back of the ring completely. This step will complete the circle of the ring, drawing both sides together tightly.

JEWELER'S TIP

TAKE CARE WHEN SNIPPING THE EDGES OF THE SCREENING MATERIAL. A CLOSE, UNFRAYED EDGE IS DESIRED, BUT IT IS EASY TO CUT INTO THE WEAVE OF THE SCREEN, POTENTIALLY UNRAVELING A ROW OF METAL.

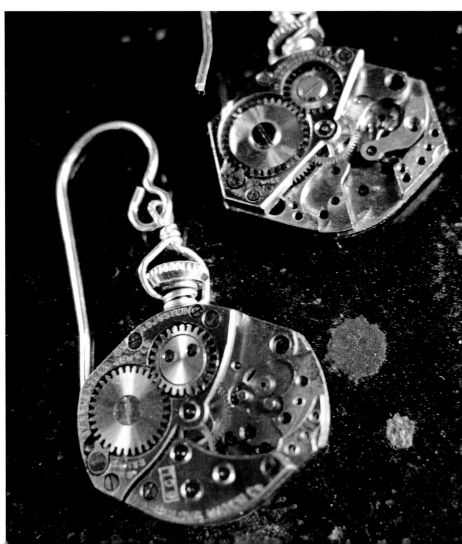

GALLERY OF JEWELRY

NAUTICAL INDICATOR NECKLACE

Indicator labels sold through nautical hardware stores inspired this design. The additional stainless steel flat and lock washers complement the sterling silver hammered chain.

RED DISK BRACELET

Red coral disks, center drilled, create a rhythm to this bracelet that is punctuated by white coin pearls and stainless steel hex nuts.

AFRICAN TRADE CUFF

The fourteenth-century trade beads are offset by stainless steel hex nuts in this modern design. The weight of the material feels substantial on the wrist, but is comfortable to wear.

LAPIS ROUNDS

The gorgeous color of the lapis and the luster of the pearls are enhanced by the shimmer of the stainless steel hex nuts.

JANGLE BRACELET

This bracelet is a signature design. Crystal nuggets accented with various bits of hardware and freshwater pearls make it a perfect party bracelet year-round.

ANTIQUE KEY CHARM BRACELET

Lost keys have a new use when used as charms. Blue and red glass beads coupled with red branch coral add color to the assorted nuts dangling from this bracelet.

PRIMARY BRACELET

Sometimes simple is better. This design combines the materials used in the more elaborate cuff bracelet in a single strand of color. It can be easily worn grouped with other hardware bracelets.

FACES OF TIME NECKLACE

Recycled round watch faces are grouped on an adjustable sterling silver chain.
A single day of the week disk dangles free from the clasp.

WATCH GEAR DANGLE EARRINGS

The internal workings of hexagonal watches are the simple foundation for these earrings.

FACES OF TIME BRACELET

Playful watch faces and small gears adorn a fluorescent green rubber
cuff bracelet.

BRASS HASP NECKLACE

A brass hasp is strung on metallic stain cord and combined with antique coral beads and brass threaded inserts. A bronze ferrule completes the design.

FLY FISHING BRACELET

Hand-tied fishing lures and heavy sinkers are added to brass hex nuts and washers on a brass chain link bracelet.

DIPSEY SWIVEL SINKER EARRINGS

Fishing sinkers are the adornment for the colorful Venetian beads on these earrings. Brass hex nuts top the design.

BARB SPLICER EARRINGS

A single, unique piece of hardware is sometimes all that is needed to create a dramatic earring. The warm tones of carnelian complement the brass color of the hardware.

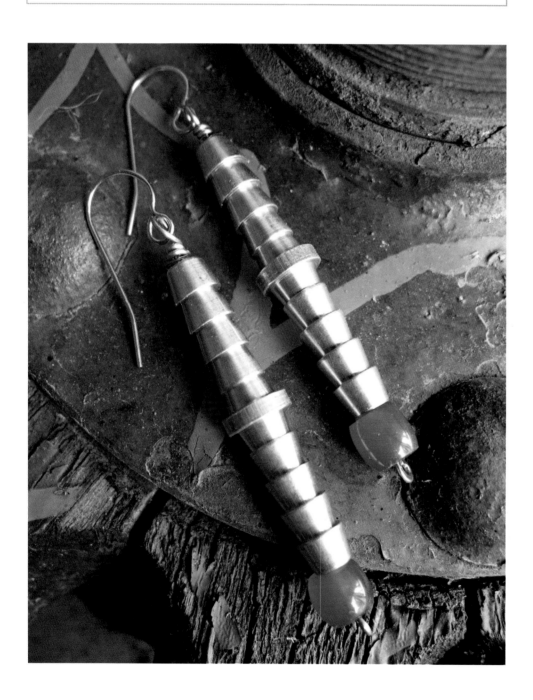

Making Designer Jewelry from Hardware, Beads, and Gems

VENETIAN MODERN GLASS

A third-generation glass designer in Venice, Italy, creates unique geometric glass beads. Coupled with square grid pearls, they accentuate the structure of the hex nuts.

RECYCLED MOTHER BOARD

The recycled parts of a computer's mother board are assembled with ball chain and hex nut accents.

COMPUTER CHIP EARRINGS

Interesting, long sections of computer board are hung simply from French ear wires.

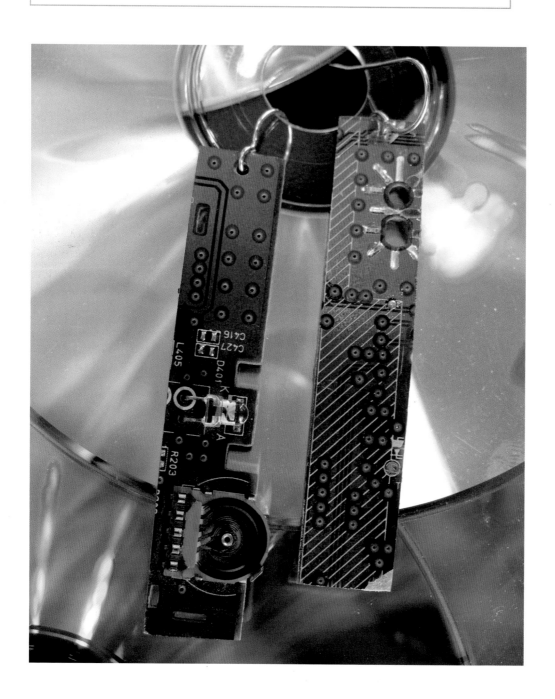

COMPUTER CHIP PENDANT

A single square of computer board is suspended on a bias from a chain made from brass beads.

MOTHER BOARD BRACELET

Hand-drilled, identical sections of computer board flip back and forth on this sterling silver and hex nut bracelet.

COMPUTER AND HEX NUT DANGLE

Matching computer board pieces are dangled from stainless steel and brass hex nut sections.

Local hardware stores were a necessary resource for this book. I cannot stress enough the need to support these individually owned enterprises; the big box stores are big competition, but cannot provide the service, atmosphere, or knowledge that these old stores offer. Be prepared to spend a lot of time discovering their hidden treasures and do not be surprised when the owners are at first wary of your interest. They generally warm up to the idea and often find all kinds of things that can be adapted to jewelry making. Online resources are also important; they have many of the miniature sizes of hardware that will be necessary for projects. I have included three that should be able to meet all your specialty hardware needs. Finally, local craft and bead stores provide a hands-on resource for the beginning jewelry maker and some of the materials you will need to add to the hardware. Jewelry-making Internet sources will help round out the inventory and also will provide the tools and supplies required.

ONLINE HARDWARE

McMaster-Carr
630.600.3600
WWW.MCMASTER.COM
Huge selection of hardware, easily searchable website with illustrations; only available online—print catalog is no longer available

Reactive Metals Studio
800.876.3434
WWW.REACTIVEMETALS.COM
Supplier of niobium and titanium for jewelry making

Small Parts, Inc.
800.220.4242
WWW.SMALLPARTS.COM
Print catalog shipped to United States and Canada only

UNITED STATES

Artgems, Inc.
480.545.6009
WWW.ARTGEMSINC.COM
Gemstones, beads, findings, and other jewelry-related supplies

Beadalon
866.423.2325
WWW.BEADALON.COM
Beading wire, wire, and general jewelry-making supplies

CGM
800.426.5246
WWW.CGMFINDINGS.COM
Wholesale wire, metal beads, and findings

CK Gems USA
212.683.0297
WWW.CKGEMSNY.COM
Large selection of gemstones

Earthstone
800.747.8088
WWW.EARTHSTONE.COM
High-quality gemstones

Fire Mountain Gems and Beads
800.355.2137
WWW.FIREMOUNTAINGEMS.COM
Large catalog of jewelry-related supplies in all categories

Halstead Bead
800.528.0535
WWW.HALSTEADBEAD.COM
Findings, metal, crystal, and other jewelry-related supplies

HHH Enterprises
800.777.0218
WWW.HHHENTERPRISES.COM
General jewelry-making supplies

MonsterSlayer
505.598.5322
WWW.MONSTERSLAYER.COM
Large selection of gemstones, beads, findings, and other jewelry-related supplies

Rings & Things
800.366.2156
WWW.RINGS-THINGS.COM
Wholesale jewelry-making supplies

Rio Grande
800.545.6566
WWW.RIOGRANDE.COM
Large catalog of jewelry-related supplies in all categories

South Pacific Wholesale Co.
800.338-2162
WWW.BEADING.COM
Pearls and stone beads

Stuller, Inc.
800.877.7777
WWW.STULLER.COM
Large catalog of jewelry-related supplies in all categories

INTERNATIONAL

AUSTRALIA

Katie's Treasures
011.61.2.4968.9485
WWW.KATIESTREASURES.COM.AU
Gemstones, beads, and jewelry-related supplies

Space Trader Beads
011.61.3.9534.6867
WWW.SPACETRADER.COM.AU
Gemstones, beads, and jewelry-related supplies

CANADA

beadFX
877.473.2323
WWW.BEADFX.COM
Gemstones, beads, crystal, and findings

Canada Beading Supply
800.291.6668
WWW.CANBEAD.COM
Large catalog of jewelry-related supplies

The House of Orange
866.401.9174
WWW.HOUSEOFORANGE.BIZ
Beads, crystal, and general jewelry-related supplies

UNITED KINGDOM

Beadgems
011.44.845.123.2743
WWW.BEADGEMS.COM
Beads, crystal, and findings

Beads Unlimited
011.44.127.374.0777
WWW.BEADSUNLIMITED.CO.UK
Supplier of beads and general jewelry-related supplies

Beadworks
011.44.208.553.3240
WWW.BEADWORKS.CO.UK
Supplier of beads and general jewelry-related supplies

Kernowcrafts Rocks & Gems Ltd.
011.44.187.257.3888
WWW.KERNOWCRAFT.COM
Beads and jewelry-related supplies

ABOUT THE AUTHOR

Nicole Noelle Sherman designs and creates jewelry in her studio in Free Union, Virginia. Her work grows out of a family tradition of art and architecture. Nicole's approach is to redefine the traditional and create unique pieces with careful attention to detail. Her Softhardwear jewelry is a modern and innovative synergy of materials combining basic hardware with interesting beads, pearls, and gemstones. Her work is available in galleries and fine jewelry stores in Virginia and New England and online through her website: www.nicolenoelle.com.

AUTHOR'S NOTE

I have taken a bit of artistic license in the introduction. Much of it is as I remember, but the character of "Papa" is really based on a neighbor of mine, Mr. Tucker, who has passed away. I never really knew either of my grandfathers (they were gone before I was old enough to remember), but if I could pick someone to be my grandfather it would be Mr. Tucker. He was kind and considerate, a man who cared more for the little things–like a chat with a neighbor–than where you came from or how important you thought you were. The memories of the time spent with him will always be with me.

ACKNOWLEDGMENTS

Thank you once again to Mary Ann Hall, acquisitions editor at Quarry Books. Without her, I would have too much time on my hands. Translating my design process and vision into a publishable manuscript has been an experience and without Mary Ann the experience would have been far less enjoyable.

Thank you again to Lyn Rushton. Lyn is the owner of Les Yeux du Monde, an art gallery in Charlottesville, Virginia, and has been my home base since the day she opened the gallery in September 2002. While I sell at many other galleries and jewelry stores, Lyn is my foundation. She is never wary of any of my explorations; she allows me the freedom and space to create.

Thank you to my children, Arianna and Porter. They are a constant source of inspiration. Many ideas have grown from their childhood imaginations and ability to look at materials in new ways: Porter, thank you for bringing me all your thoughts and bits from your shop in the basement, and Arianna, thank you for being such an imaginative thinker. Thank you to my mother for having faith, being fun, and nurturing my imagination. Thank you to my sisters, Anne and Lisa, for being my first, sometimes my only, and certainly my best customers. And finally, thank you to my architect husband Bill for supporting me and encouraging me to think outside the box, for allowing me to raid his shop, and finally teaching me not to be afraid of power tools.